What others are

"This is a must read! Inte
developed for all readers a very useful banking tool."
— *Dr. J. Mark Dufner, President*
The Memory Company, Inc.

"Ken's book takes the mystery and fear out of borrowing money. It is written in layman's language and I found it to be informative and entertaining."
— *Fred Stone, Former District Director*
Small Business Administration

"A terrific primer full of humor and good common sense for any borrower. Ken lays out straight forward text on how to maintain the banker relationship, and it contains a generous portion of sound business advice for the entrepreneur as well!"
— *Walt Moeling*
Powell, Goldstein, Frazer & Murphy

"Ken's provocative style and entertaining presentation stimulates all of us outside of the formal banking community to read another chapter."
— *Floyd A. Falany, Ed.D.*
President, Reinhardt College

"An entertaining and common sense approach to banking, full of sound advice for any borrower. Certainly a valuable source of insight on how to build and maintain a successful relationship with your banker."
— *Dr. Donald Ratajczak*
Economic Forecasting Center, Georgia State University

"An invaluable asset to small and emerging business owners, prospective entrepreneurs and anyone interested in understanding the motives of bankers. Ken has combined more than two decades of experience into a comprehensive tool of "portables" that will arm current and future clients with the insights they need to build a more convincing proposal for their bankers."
— *Timothy S. Mescon, Ph.D.*
Dean, Michael J. Coles School of Business, Kennesaw State College

"A strong personal relationship with your banker is critical to the success of any business. In his book, Ken shares an easy step-by-step approach on exactly how to develop that winning relationship."
–*Jimmy Ray Waldron*
Former Executive Vice President, The Limited Stores, Inc.

HOW TO MAKE YOUR BANKER SAY YES!

50 Specific Strategies For Guaranteed Loan Approval

By T. Ken Driskell

POWER**BANKING**
PUBLICATIONS

A Division Of **P**OWER**BANKING** PARTNERS

How To Make Your Banker Say Yes!

50 Specific Strategies For Guaranteed Loan Approval

By: T. Ken Driskell

Published by:	PowerBanking Publications P.O. Box 707 Alpharetta, Georgia 30239-0707 (770) 569-8416
Edited by:	Precision Communications (770) 386-5373
Design, Illustrations and Layout by:	TMP Publishing Company (770) 606-1721

Copyright © 1996 By T. Ken Driskell

All rights reserved. No part of this book may be reproduced or transmitted in any form or by any means, electronic or mechanical, including photocopying, recording or by any information storage and retrieval systems without written permission from the author, except for the inclusion of brief quotations in a review.

Library of Congress Catalog Card Number 96-69021
ISBN: 0-9653204-9-9
Printed in the U.S.A.

FOREWORD

It has become commonplace these days to speak about the many changes that are occurring in our society. It is true that dramatic and revolutionary changes are taking place across the entire spectrum of American business. These fast-moving changes are occurring largely because of increased competition, the emergence of a global economy and rapid technological advances. The banking industry certainly has not been immune to these changes. In fact, banking may have been affected even more than others and is now as competitive as any other business in the United States. The transformation of banking from a staid, highly regulated industry to a more creative and innovative one has produced many benefits for the banks themselves, the economy and most of their customers. On the negative side, however, not all bank customers have profited from these changes in the banking industry. Because of the increasing sophistication of many banks and bankers, it is now more essential than ever that both parties to a banking relationship understand the needs of the other if that relationship is to be successful and profitable.

Ken Driskell, in his entertaining and insightful new book, provides many of the solutions to the problems that borrowers and lenders face when attempting to negotiate credit terms. In clear, down-to-earth, humorous language, he sets out common sense rules to be followed by bankers and customers alike. These rules are based on his long and extensive experience as a banker, businessman and community leader. This is a long overdue book that needs to be read by bankers who can benefit from his advice on how to provide quality service to their customers and a productive working environment for their employees. It should also be required reading for bank customers who want to overcome the hurdles of the credit extension process and to achieve a happy relationship with a financial institution.

As a former central banker who has observed banks in action for many years, I am confident that anyone who follows Ken Driskell's 50 strategies for guaranteed loan approval will find that any banker will be happy to say "yes" to their banking requests.

— Robert P. Forrestal
Former President, Federal Reserve Bank of Atlanta
Chairman, Banking Practice Group
Smith, Gambrell and Russell

Table of Contents

PART ONE

Chapter One 17
   "I Need That In Small Bills"
Chapter Two 19
   Get Out Of Your Box
Chapter Three 21
   Man Overboard!
Chapter Four 23
   The First Colony Bank Oath
Chapter Five 25
   "Don't Let The Little Picture Eat Your Lunch"
Chapter Six 29
   Risk Analyzers
Chapter Seven 31
   Does This Sound Like You?
Chapter Eight 33
   Or Is This You?
Chapter Nine 35
   Or Maybe This Is You?

PART TWO

Chapter Ten 41
   Til Death Do Us Part
Chapter Eleven 43
   Daddy Sent Me
Chapter Twelve 47
   Name Calling Pays Off
Chapter Thirteen 49
   If Borrowing Money Is So Great,
   Why Do I Feel So Depressed?
Chapter Fourteen 51
   I Wasn't Wearing Anything But A Smile
Chapter Fifteen 55
   It's Expensive But It's Worth It
Chapter Sixteen 59
   A One-Liner Guaranteed To Make You A Living Legend

Chapter Seventeen 63
   You're So Hot
Chapter Eighteen 65
   Don't Pick A Bank, Pick A Banker
Chapter Nineteen 69
   Am I Starting-Up Or Backing-Up?
Chapter Twenty 73
   I Don't Look That Old…But I Do Have That Much Experience
Chapter Twenty-one 77
   I Need To See Something In XXL
Chapter Twenty-two 79
   Whatever!
Chapter Twenty-three 83
   "Turn The Lights Down, I'm Coming Right Over"
Chapter Twenty-four 85
   Please Go With Me!
Chapter Twenty-five 87
   Need It By 5…I Gotta Make Payroll
Chapter Twenty-six 89
   Hey Guys! Please Don't Eat At Your Desk Today
Chapter Twenty-seven 91
   All Right, It's Show Time!
Chapter Twenty-eight 95
   Am I In The Right Place?
Chapter Twenty-nine 99
   Show Me Yours, I'll Show You Mine
Chapter Thirty 101
   If Borrowing Money Is So Easy, Why Is My Life So Difficult?
Chapter Thirty-one 103
   The Bank Carried Me Longer Than Momma Did
Chapter Thirty-two 107
   I Need A Loan, Not A Lecture
Chapter Thirty-three 109
   My Car Got Repossessed…I'm On My Feet Again
Chapter Thirty-four 113
   Don't Laugh…I Really Owe This Much

Chapter Thirty-five 117
Does Mine Look Pitiful?
Chapter Thirty-six 119
Supplying Financial Information
Chapter Thirty-seven 121
I Don't Need To Stop And Ask Directions
Chapter Thirty-eight 123
I've Never Proposed To Anyone Before
Chapter Thirty-nine 125
Sometimes It Just Don't Add Up
Chapter Forty 127
This Little Piggy Had A Plan
Chapter Forty-one 131
No, Not Yet, I Said
Chapter Forty-two 133
If Borrowing Money Is Such A Pain, Why Do I Feel So Good?
Chapter Forty-three 137
Do What I Say, Not What I Do
Chapter Forty-four 141
Explain That To Me One More Time
Chapter Forty-five 143
Exactly How Did You Get This Job?
Chapter Forty-six 145
You Wanna Go Out Sometime?
Chapter Forty-seven 149
Take My Kids...Please!
Chapter Forty-eight 152
The Bank And Your Spouse Will Be Happy
Chapter Forty-nine 155
Okay! Okay! My Word Is My Bond
Chapter Fifty 157
Cash Is King And I Feel Like A Joker
Chapter Fifty-one 161
I'm So Flexible I Can Put My Foot In My Mouth
Chapter Fifty-two 163
Plastic Won't Float Forever

Chapter Fifty-three 167
   Stay In Touch With Yours
Chapter Fifty-four 171
   Say What?!
Chapter Fifty-five 173
   Don't Talk Ugly
Chapter Fifty-six 175
   I'm Not A Non-Profit...I Just Look Like One
Chapter Fifty-seven 177
   Did You Say Bored Or Board?
Chapter Fifty-eight 181
   Only If You Let Me Buy
Chapter Fifty-nine 185
   Tell Me One More Time How Good I Am
Review 188
Index 194

WARNING - DISCLAIMER

This book is designed to provide information on how to develop and maintain good banking relationships. Please be advised that the author and PowerBanking Publications are not involved in rendering legal, accounting or other professional services. Consult a competent professional if you need legal advice or other expert assistance.

Every effort has been made to make this book as complete and accurate as possible. However, mistakes may exist. Therefore, this text should be used only as a general guide and not as the ultimate source for managing banking relationships.

The purpose of this book is to educate and entertain. The author and PowerBanking Publications shall have neither liability nor responsibility to any person or entity with respect to any loss or damage caused or alleged to be caused directly or indirectly by the information contained in this book.

ABOUT THE AUTHOR

T. Ken Driskell is a banker, business owner, community leader, speaker, writer and (would you believe) stand-up comic. He is President, CEO and co-founder of First Colony Bank, which recently received the "Quality Service Award" for the most outstanding customer service among banks in Georgia. Ken serves on the Board of Directors for numerous profit and non-profit organizations and actively volunteers time to his local government.

For more than twenty-three years, Ken has been lending money to business owners for start-ups, acquisitions and expansions. Not only does Ken actively counsel and consult with business owners, but he operates his own successful business as well, putting into practice the same ideas he so freely passes along to his customers.

As an expert in the area of business lending, Ken summarizes in this book hundreds of "secrets" you can use to get your next loan approved.

DEDICATED TO
THE MEMORY OF MY BEST FRIEND,
LEON KING.

PART ONE

SETTING THE STAGE

CHAPTER 1

"I Need That In Small Bills"

"Put $100,000 in my briefcase or I will blow up the building."

It all began when a young well-dressed man with a briefcase walked into the branch office and asked for the branch manager. "May we step into your office?" he asked.

As they sat there, it became obvious to Roxanne that this guy had on heavy makeup and a wig. Dark sunglasses prevented a good look at his eyes. His hands were small and delicate. He wore no jewelry. His facial features were also small. Maybe this was a woman dressed like a man!

He spoke emotionally about the political unrest in a foreign country. Needing money to help with his cause, he demanded that Roxanne put $100,000 in small bills in his briefcase and no one would be hurt. Otherwise, he would trigger a bomb he had planted on the roof of the building. He pointed to the detonator in his briefcase.

As coolly as possible, Roxanne got up from her office chair and made her way across the lobby to the teller line. On her way, she gave her assistant the sign that says, "Hey, I'm in trouble but don't call the police yet. We don't want this guy to get trapped in here with us."

With knees knocking, Roxanne went behind the teller line and opened a cash drawer. She grabbed about $10,000 in fives and tens. Hoping for her life that two huge fistfuls of cash would satisfy the thief, Roxanne returned to her office and dropped the money in his briefcase. He stood up, thanked her and left the bank.

Someone needs to teach this guy the right way to apply for a loan!

One month later the same fellow hit another area bank. Two months later he was chased down at his home where he was burning the remaining evidence (the money) in his back yard. From all appearances, he obviously didn't know how to invest wisely, either.

GET OUT OF YOUR BOX

I started my banking career in 1973. That same year I took a real estate licensing course. I did not do this because I wanted to be a real estate agent (in fact I didn't even take the exam), but because I wanted to understand the realtor's needs. As a banker who was closing many real estate transactions, it was easier to satisfy the agents' needs and concerns if I knew what they were.

Over the years, I have continued to use this approach to understand my customers' needs. Not long ago our bank decided to solicit more banking business from the medical community, so I attended a two-day conference for physicians and their vendors. Through seminars and networking, I discovered many things that physicians expect from their bankers.

In 1995, I took a stand-up comedy class. Not because of some secret desire to become a stand-up comedian, but because I wanted to learn how to use more humor in my corporate speaking opportunities. This learning experience definitely helped me to be more relaxed at the podium. I now tell all young business professionals that the "power of the podium" is the most effective business skill they can develop. Effective public speaking is a powerful talent that most people are scared to develop, but if you do, it will open doors for you.

Always stretch yourself to grow and develop - it is a lifelong exercise. I had been in banking for twenty-two years when I took my first comedy class. It might not appear that comedy and banking have much in common; however, the class had a significant impact on both my personal and professional life.

Come on! Get out of your box!

CHAPTER 3

MAN OVERBOARD!

Even though I am a banker, I feel a strong camaraderie with business owners and entrepreneurs. With a wife and two small children, I left a secure banking job in 1984 to start a new bank.

I will never forget the morning I turned in my resignation at 8:00 a.m. At 8:05 a.m., I was back in my driveway, thinking, "I must be crazy. I'm going to start a new bank?" I had no building, no land, no customers, no employees - I didn't even have government approval! But I did have the support of some other key people, and I knew what had to be done.

If you have ever started your own business, significantly expanded a small one, or purchased an existing business, you understand this emotional roller coaster feeling. The ability to enjoy the entrepreneurial spirit through a free enterprise system is a real rush!

I had that rush! I felt like I could do anything. With a positive mental attitude, I knew that everything would be okay.

" The power of the podium is the most effective business skill you can develop. "

THE FIRST COLONY BANK OATH

A few years ago, our institution adopted the First Colony Bank Oath. I believe this idea actually evolved from one of our customer service representatives, a member of an in-house marketing committee. The oath goes like this:

"At First Colony Bank I will bend over backwards to make my customer know that his or her business is important... every customer, every time."

Studies from this marketing committee determined that we should focus on our people, who impact the quality of our customer service. We are constantly training them, looking for unique ways to keep attitude and morale high. An oath of service was a perfect tie-in to our efforts.

We printed the oaths on sheets of paper, rolled them up diploma-style, and tied them with burgundy ribbon. I addressed my staff at a morning meeting, draped in a judge's robe for a little added dramatic emphasis. As I handed each employee his or her oath, I asked them to stand up, raise their right hand and repeat after me as I recited the oath. I then asked them to sign and date the oath, with all documents to be placed in their personnel file.

The ceremony had been a lot of fun up to this point, but now the group realized there was a real point being made. "Hey, this signed statement is going to our personnel file and we will really be held accountable to deliver quality customer service," employees quickly gathered. "We are expected to go that extra mile, to really 'bend over backwards' to help our customers."

For months after that meeting, I would wander through the bank and casually ask an employee to recite the oath. If they recited the oath correctly, I would hand them a crisp five-dollar bill and tell them to have lunch on the bank. After I did that the first time, it was amazing how fast everyone memorized the oath. Everywhere I looked, I saw copies of the oath posted in employee work stations. Two years later, our bank won the "Quality Service Award" from among all competing banks in our state.

CHAPTER 5

Don't Let The Little Picture Eat Your Lunch

One of our bank tellers entered the branch manager's office one morning. "There's a customer out here that I don't think I can 'bend over backwards' for," she said.

It definitely was a difficult-to-serve customer, the manager silently agreed as the name was mentioned. In fact, he was the kind you hated to see coming because you could never do anything right for him. The branch manager consoled the teller, assured her that we should do our best, and sent her back to the teller line.

When the branch manager came to me to relay the story, I realized that the "oath" definitely had made an impact on our employees. I also realized that our obstinate customer represented a real problem for several bank employees with his repeated phone calls and ridiculous requests.

I asked the branch manager to send a memo to the entire staff, requesting that all further calls from this customer be directed to me, regardless of the reason - even a balance inquiry on his checking account. When the manager left my office, I picked up the phone and called our customer. I proceeded to tell him how much we appreciated his business and that as President of the bank I personally wanted him to know that we considered him to be a most valued customer. I told him I wanted to be his personal banker and for him to ask directly for me anytime he called the bank.

I didn't hear from him for two months. He didn't even want to discuss any bank "problems," but wanted to relay his recent investments in the stock market and get my insights on them. This customer never had any real problems; he just wanted to be noticed, to receive some signal of appreciation. As soon as he became aware that quality service was available to him from none other than the President of the bank, he was completely satisfied. I might hear from him now once every six months or so.

The lesson here is: As owners or officers of our companies, we must stay in touch with our employees out there on the firing line. A problem situation that becomes accepted as normal by employees may also be one that can be easily cleared up by the owner. In this situation, my actions increased my employees' productivity by freeing them to do other things. By not having to deal with the ranting and raving of the obstinate customer, they enjoyed a decreased stress level as well. As owners and managers, we can't get too concerned with the big picture. If we do, the little picture will eat our lunch.

❝ **My loan was approved...** ❞
I got thirty years.

❝ **It is always easy to borrow** ❞
money when you don't need it.

CHAPTER 6

RISK ANALYZERS

One of the fundamentals of business is how to make the most money while taking the least amount of risk. Banks make money by earning interest on the loans they make. Therefore, banks want to make loans that carry the least amount of risk.

You should think of bankers as "risk analyzers." They evaluate many loan applications and choose to approve those loans which seem to have the least amount of risk. Of course, there is some degree of risk associated with any loan that is made, even those secured with cash. Several years ago we had a defaulted loan that was secured by a cash account with a large brokerage firm. Because of suits and counter suits, it took us two years to get our money through the courts.

Bankers analyze four things when determining your degree of risk:
1) Your character
2) Your credit history
3) The collateral offered
4) Your capacity to repay

In understanding this approach, you must appear "less risky" than most borrowers. The strategies in this book will help position you to be selected as "the most likely to repay." When this happens, you are guaranteed loan approval.

CHAPTER 7

DOES THIS SOUND LIKE YOU?

I've been in corporate sales for seventeen years. I've moved six times. I'm in a town now that I really like but I don't know anybody. I don't even know my neighbors. I jump on a plane on Monday morning and fly back in on Friday night. I spend the weekends being a part time dad, working in the yard and filling out my expense report. I have no sense of identity with this community. I wish I did. I want my kids to have a place they can call home. I don't want them to change schools anymore.

I think I'll leave my corporate job and go into the consulting business. Or I might just buy a local business that's been around for a while. Maybe I'll start a local business. I can think of several that should do well around here. How do I start? I don't really know any of the local business people.

Try this!

Go to your local bank. Ask to be introduced to the bank president or one of the senior lending officers, in most cases an older, more experienced banker who has been in the area for a very long time. He will know most of the local business owners.

Sit with this experienced banker and tell him your story. Ask for help in finding a local business for sale or what types of start-up businesses are needed in the community.

Why will he be eager to help you? He wants to lend you money. You look like a good risk. You have held a stable job for seventeen years. You have a good nest egg saved up. You have great experience in sales and marketing. Your work ethics are great and your credit history is perfect. Believe me, he wants to meet you. So go find yourself a local banker and the next time your corporate employer asks you to move to another city you can say, "No thanks, I have my own plans this time."

CHAPTER 8

OR IS THIS YOU?

You started working for her five years ago when she opened her first boutique. Now she has two stores and total sales are over $3 million a year. You know that she is netting about 8% after taxes and that is after she takes out a very generous salary for herself. Lately she has been spending a lot less time at the store.

Fortunately, she can rely on you to keep the place straight. You could actually run the place if she never showed up again. You're better with the customers than she is. You certainly know them better than she does. But you got a nice raise when you came to work for her and she's always good to you with a nice year end bonus.

Nevertheless, you keep having the same nagging thoughts. "If she can do this I know I can. She's not any smarter than me. Why should I be working for $40,000 a year while she's making $340,000? I'm working hard and she's getting rich. I should start my own business just like she did!"

66 **The only way to continue growing is to stretch yourself.** 99

66 **It's easy to get your loan approved when your ski mask completely disguises your true identity.** 99

CHAPTER 9

OR MAYBE THIS IS YOU?

You have been working very hard for years to build your business to where it is today. Long hours, no vacation, no days off, little time at home with the kids. Many sacrifices have been made all for the sake of building something of value to help support your family and hopefully to provide that much-needed source of retirement income.

You are very proud of what you have done with the company in the first few years. Sales are up and the future looks very bright. You suddenly realize that you simply do not have adequate cash available to grow the company to its fullest potential. How frustrating to have more business than you can handle!

This situation takes place all the time in businesses both large and small. It happens in start-up businesses, where it is common to have orders in hand without the necessary working capital to fill them.

What can you do? Your rich aunt has plenty of money; however, borrowing from relatives can turn into an uncomfortable situation. Family gatherings can be awkward, especially if you have a problem making the payments on time.

You could bring in a partner to provide the cash that is so desperately needed. But then what happens? Suddenly you don't own 100% of the company. Now you own 50% and your partner owns 50%. This can require a delicate balancing act. Whether it's a silent partner or a managing partner, his or her influence and input must still be considered. This situation can create significant conflict regarding the growth and direction of what was once your company.

You could seek the financial resources of a venture capital firm. The big hurdle here is convincing the principals that you have a viable product or service. If they finally do agree to invest, you may find their control and influence to be even greater than that of a silent or managing partner.

Well, what about your local bank? You have been going in and out of there two or three times a week for years, but you really don't know anyone except the head teller. Why not develop a relationship with your local banker and borrow the money you need from him? You will retain 100% of the ownership of the business that you have worked so hard to develop. Your banker now becomes your financial partner; however, all of the equity in the company still belongs to you.

What can you do to "Make Your Banker Say Yes" when you need to borrow money? That's what you are about to learn in this book.

As President and CEO of a community bank with twenty-three years of experience, I am about to share with you some enormously valuable insights from the banker's point of view. These ideas are guaranteed to work. Most can produce results immediately. Others will take a little more time to develop. Make the investment. These ideas will get your next loan request approved.

Let us continue as I share with you fifty powerful strategies you can use to make **your** banker say "yes!"

PART TWO

50 SPECIFIC STRATEGIES FOR GUARANTEED LOAN APPROVAL

◆

CHAPTER 10

TIL DEATH DO US PART

I had been trying for about a year to get David to move his business to my bank. He finally agreed to make the switch. After the last loan closed, he walked into my office. Standing in the doorway, he looked me straight in the eye and said, "I've moved all my business to your bank. I even moved my kids' accounts here. I will refer all my friends to you. I am going to be a loyal customer. You better take good care of me."

With those words he sent me on an emotional roller coaster. On the one hand I was happy that I had finally landed a new account that I had worked hard to get. On the other hand, I was concerned about what would happen if someday I had to turn him down on a loan or not handle a specific request.

This same man will introduce me in a crowd saying, "This is my banker. He takes really good care of me, too." This guy is like a walking billboard for me. If I indeed do take good care of him, I have a customer for life.

I always do three things for this customer:
1. I always take his phone calls or else call him back immediately.
2. If he needs to see me, I juggle my calendar.
3. If he needs money, I help him shape his loan request so I feel confident about its approval.

Why do I feel such a responsibility to this man? Because he is continuously stressing his genuine loyalty to me privately and publicly.

You should feel comfortable looking your banker straight in the eye and saying, "I am going to be a loyal customer. You better take care of me and be there when I need you."

Specific Strategy # 1

**Tell your banker
that you will be a loyal customer.**

CHAPTER 11

DADDY SENT ME

As a banker, I love to hear a new customer come in and say, "My friend sent me here," especially if that friend is a good bank customer. Any businessman will agree that the best prospect is one who is referred by a satisfied customer. So when you approach your banker, who do you want to be? You want to be a referral from a satisfied customer of the bank.

Do some homework. Talk to your friends at work, at church, anywhere you go. Approach a friend whom you know to be successful and in good financial condition. Ask him where he banks. Tell him you are looking for a good banker. If he is happy with his banker, he will certainly let you know. Bingo! Now, you can tell your banker that you were referred to him by a satisfied customer of the bank.

Your banker suddenly begins to feel comfortable with you. He knows your friend to be a very good customer of the bank who is honest, hardworking and successful. Your banker will associate you with these same characteristics unless you give him reason to believe differently.

Be careful when you do your homework on this point. You do not want to be a referral by someone from whom the bank may have recently repossessed their vehicle. You do not want to be a referral by someone who is known by your banker to have poor credit.

Just use one good solid name as a referral. Don't be a name dropper. Bankers totally ignore that approach and you don't build credibility by attempting it.

If you are new to your area and have not met anyone, read the newspaper. Check the paid ads, let an ad refer you, and tell your banker so. Advertising is expensive, and it is often difficult to monitor its effectiveness. A banker will appreciate the fact that the ads are working.

Specific Strategy # 2

It is best to be referred to the bank by a satisfied customer.

THE $1.6 MILLION DOLLAR CAR WASH

I decided to try and squeeze in a car wash during my lunch hour. I pulled into line at the car wash behind Mark, a friend who worked in administration at a local hospital.

As we stood in the parking lot, Mark introduced me to a friend of his (also in the car wash line) who was in the children's day care business. We exchanged business cards.

Two days later, I followed up on this new person to discover he and his wife were looking to move their business to a local bank.

Within sixty days, we had approved a $700,000 loan to refinance one of the couple's existing centers and another loan for $900,000 for new construction. A total of $1.6 million in loans all because I decided to squeeze in a car wash.

Ever since that day, I always make sure to follow up on every lead I get.

> **If you network in a genuine and sincere manner, new business will pile up on your doorstep.**

> **Effective networking is the process of creating relationships whereby you help others achieve their goals which in turn helps you achieve yours.**

CHAPTER 12

NAME CALLING PAYS OFF

Hundreds of times, I have had a new customer walk into my bank and say, "I'm here because they treat me like a number down the street. I've banked there for ten years and they have no idea who I am." We all have names and we like to hear people call our name.

If this is true for you, then it is also true for bank employees, particularly tellers and customer service representatives. Learn these employees' names and use them as often as possible. Why? These people have a lot of conversations with the lending officers at the bank. Some positive comments from them to your loan officer will certainly do you no harm. The best way for you to help generate such comments is to know these personnel by name and to generate pleasant conversation with them as often as possible.

You should identify other ways that you can personalize your relationship with the bank. One idea is to take a basket of goodies with your name or business card attached to your bank on holidays. Your gift will find its way to the bank's kitchen table, where it will stay front and center during coffee and lunch times. Your name and your thoughtful gift will be mentioned many times by most of the bank's personnel during the next few days. Whatever you spend on the gift will be outweighed by the goodwill it creates for you at the bank.

If you happen to see a news article regarding any bank personnel (particularly if it includes a picture), cut it out and mail it to that person with a short note saying something like, "Congratulations! Extra copy for your scrapbook!"

Many times, my opinion of a customer has been influenced by glowing remarks made by a teller in general conversation. So, out with the numbers, and in with the names! Use it to your benefit!

Specific Strategy # 3

**Always call tellers
and other employees by name.**

CHAPTER 13

IF BORROWING MONEY IS SO GREAT, WHY DO I FEEL SO DEPRESSED?

Regardless of what your circumstances may be at the time, you must be up for any meeting with your banker. You have to go in with a big smile, a lot of eye contact and a great optimistic attitude. If you look and act confident, your banker is more likely to have confidence in you.

You can control the tone of the meeting much more than you think. All you have to do is set a positive stage. For example, if you say, "You may not be able to help me, because National Bank down the street turned me down last week," then you have made it easy for your banker to say "no." How about "I've got a great business, a great product and I want to tell you all about it. If you approve my loan, I'm prepared to move all of my business to your bank, including my business accounts and my personal accounts." Which opening line do you think will interest your banker more?

If you talk in a negative manner and give negative opinions on issues, then you are bound to leave a negative impression with your banker. Don't do this. The way in which you present yourself is typically how you are perceived. If you are continuously complaining about your financial problems, or talking about your poor health, then others always will associate you with these negative aspects. On the other hand, if you are always positive and mentioning the good things that are happening to you, then others will see you as a well-adjusted, successful person. This is exactly the perception you want your banker to have of you.

Does this mean that you avoid talking about your problems? Of course not. You identify them and talk enthusiastically and confidently about the ways you plan to solve them.

Specific Strategy # 4

You must present yourself as an assertive and confident person with good communication skills.

CHAPTER 14

I Wasn't Wearing Anything But A Smile

Body language is very important, and the nonverbal cues you send certainly will be read by your banker. You should appear relaxed, calm and confident. Put on a comfortable smile.

If your bank officer picks up any sign of anxiety on your part, he should respond by putting you at ease. Very successful business people have come into my office to request a loan, only to get so nervous as to the point of hyperventilation. When I notice any sign of anxiety from a customer, I try to do most of the talking. Perhaps then my customer will begin to breathe again!

Remember to breathe slowly and you will remain calm. You must keep blood and oxygen going to the old brain. You don't want to pass out right there on the bank floor, do you?

The most important thing you wear is your smile. The expression on your face makes more of an impact than any article of clothing. A smile, like a picture, is worth a thousand words. Be assertive, speak clearly and maintain good eye contact, especially when making key points. Your banker will assume, and rightly so, that the communication skills used during your interview are the same ones you use with your employees, your vendors, and your associates. Your basic communication skills are a valuable asset to the success of your company. This asset is weighed by the banker when analyzing the risk associated with your loan request.

Specific Strategy # 5

A smile is your most valuable asset.

BANK NOTES

"Don't Be Looking At Me That Way"

As business owners, we are constantly trying to identify the most effective sales tools we need to "close the sale."

Believe it or not, the most powerful sales tool we have doesn't cost anything - not one cent. We don't have to pick up the phone and order several boxes of it. We don't have to keep it stored on a shelf in the supply room or continuously check our inventory levels.

In fact, there's an unlimited supply. Why don't we use it more often?

It is literally right under our nose!

A smile!

**" A Customer Will Always "
Pick The Teller With The
Biggest Smile!**

CHAPTER 15

IT'S EXPENSIVE BUT IT'S WORTH IT

Divorce, marital separation, or rumors about either will not help your chances of receiving loan approval. Many times, divorce seems to act as a catalyst to financial ruin, drug use, job loss, depression . . . all of which can affect your income and consequently your ability to repay your loan.

If you are recently divorced or in the middle of a divorce, talk openly with your banker about your situation. Divorce, like death, can have a significant impact on the repayment of outstanding loans. Convince your banker that even in the midst of a divorce, you do have control of your financial affairs. Assure him that this situation will not affect the timely repayment of loans. Discuss in detail about the financial arrangements that are being made between you and your soon-to-be ex-spouse. Remember, you want to do everything possible to present yourself as a good risk.

Good communication skills are critical. If you can effectively communicate with your spouse during divorce proceedings, then your banker will assume that you will do the same with him during the life of the loan.

Don't have your banker guessing about your marital status or your living arrangements. He will be more comfortable with you as a credit risk if you are open and candid in these matters. Go ahead and clear them up in your first meeting.

Specific Strategy # 6

Be open and candid about your marital status or living arrangements.

TAKE MY WIFE

"I want to speak to the president of the bank," he screamed over the telephone. "You have a major problem at your bank. I just got my bank statement and there are eight canceled checks totaling $4,000 that I did not sign. Someone forged my signature on these checks and I want you to immediately put that $4,000 back into my account!"

I explained, "Sir, you need to come to the bank and sign an affidavit of forgery. And of course we will expect you to cooperate with our investigation as we apprehend, prosecute and lock up in jail whoever performed this terrible crime!"

He paused, "If I sign that affidavit thing, will you put that $4,000 back into my account?"

"Yes sir," I said. "And tell me, do you have any idea who forged your signature on those checks?"

He took a long pause, then said, "I think it was . . . my wife." He continued, "Tell me sir, are you really gonna lock my wife up in jail if I sign that affidavit?"

"Yes sir," I replied in a manner-of-fact tone.

"Then I'll be there in about five minutes," he responded.

" Make an unforgettable "
impression in thirty seconds
or less.
SMILE BIG!

" Not smiling is like having "
a million dollars in your checking
account but you're out of checks.

CHAPTER 16

A ONE-LINER GUARANTEED TO MAKE YOU A LIVING LEGEND

"How can I be a better customer?"

If you lay this one-liner on your banker, I guarantee you he will never forget you. He will also be speechless because I am sure no one has ever asked him this question before.

Think about it. When was the last time one of your customers called you on the phone and said, "Hey, how can I be a better customer?"

If you want to set the tone for the relationship you will enjoy with your banker, use this line. While your banker is picking himself up off the floor and trying to collect his thoughts, tell him you could do a few of the following:

1. Provide quality banking referrals, as well as personal introductions to them.

59

2. Make all loan payments on time.
3. Renew any necessary loans well in advance of maturity.
4. Offer updated business plans and budgets.
5. Discuss immediately any negative company trends.
6. Respond promptly to requests for financial information.

Get the idea? You finish the list. How can I be a better customer? What a powerful question! Use it with care.

Specific Strategy # 7

How can I be a better customer?

SUMMARY

Strategy # 1

Tell your banker that you will be a loyal customer.

Strategy # 2

It is best to be referred to the bank by a satisfied customer.

Strategy # 3

Always call tellers and other employees by name.

Strategy # 4

You must present yourself as an assertive and confident person with good communication skills.

Strategy # 5

A smile is your most valuable asset.

Strategy # 6

Be open and candid about your marital status or living arrangements.

Strategy # 7

How can I be a better customer?

> **Successful business owners are natural-born decision makers.**

> **I literally started this bank from the trunk of my car. I was destined to be a bank president or a tire changer.**

CHAPTER 17

You're So Hot

Bankers like to lend money to people who have a passion for what they do. Passionate and committed borrowers represent less risk. When hard times hit, a borrower who is totally committed to a successful business will hang in there until the bitter end. A borrower who does not share this passion will bail out early.

How do you convince your banker that you have a passion for what you do? You can't, so don't even try. When you talk about something that you really believe in, anyone will be able to see it in your eyes and hear it in your voice.

Successful companies have a passion for what they do. It starts at the top and spreads like a disease throughout the entire company. This type of excitement breeds high employee morale. Employees enjoy being associated with passionate, energetic, successful companies. And customers enjoy doing business with companies who have passionate and energetic employees.

Spend enough time with your banker for him to identify your passion for what you do!

Specific Strategy # 8

Have passion and commitment for what you do.

CHAPTER 18

Don't Pick A Bank, Pick A Banker

Banking is a relationship business. A bank is a physical structure made of bricks and mortar. A banker is a living person who works in a bank. You cannot have a relationship with a building, but you can have a relationship with a person. So, please give careful consideration to picking your banker.

For the most part, all banks offer the same services. No matter their size, regional banks, community banks, state banks, and national banks all provide the same basic array of products and services. Like the old adage says, "It's what inside that counts." And what's inside a bank is a banker. And like any other industry or profession, there are good bankers and not-so-good bankers. You want to pick a good one and stick with your choice.

You may be saying, "Hey, there is a difference between big banks and small banks." I agree. As a community banker for the past twenty-three years, I could write an entire book about the advantages of dealing with community banks. I am not saying, however, that you would not be happy with a large bank. I am merely suggesting that choosing the right banker is more important than choosing the right bank. A small bank may offer a quick response time to your questions, while a large bank may have a higher loan limit.

One very important point is to make sure that your chosen banker is the one who presents your request to the loan committee. You will be much better represented at a committee meeting by the banker who has personally met with you and is the same person you have chosen for a long-term banking relationship.

Look for a banker who can grow with you. You want stability, so choose a banker who you feel will not be "moving on." It takes too long to establish your relationship. You don't want it to end abruptly because of frequent transfers or moves.

Specific Strategy # 9

Don't pick a bank, pick a banker.

"A Doctor, A Preacher And A Banker"

I once had an older customer tell me that his daddy told him he should find three people to stick with for his entire life - a doctor, a preacher and a banker. "You get to know them well, son, and between the three of them, they will take good care of you," he recalled.

I recently called on a new prospect to solicit his banking business. As a very successful real estate developer and commercial builder, this fellow had been fortunate to enjoy a few excellent relationships with bankers over his forty years of business operations. However, through bank merger, acquisition and forced retirement, he now finds himself without someone he can consider his personal banker. This situation has created a hardship for him and his company. He must now take the time to chronicle the history of his business to a new banker who is not familiar with him or his company.

" Dear, Do You Think We Will Hear About Out Loan Today? "

AM I STARTING-UP OR BACKING-UP?

What is a start-up? It is when you start with nothing and build your own company. No customers, no products or services, no suppliers, no employees, no location. Get the picture?

Many start-ups literally begin in the basement of a home and eventually outgrow it. You probably know of at least one successful company that started from a basement.

New business start-ups represent a higher credit risk to banks than existing business. If you are applying for a start-up business loan, there are some things you need to do to improve your chances for approval. Your odds are not as good as those of an existing business, so you must concentrate on convincing your banker that you are an acceptable risk.

Remember that bankers are risk analyzers. This is what they do for a living. A successful banker (and you definitely want to choose a successful one!) must be right 99% of the time. This means he can only make a "bad" loan 1% of the time. This is a tough standard to maintain and requires a significant amount of due diligence when analyzing numerous loan requests.

What can you do to make this analysis an easier process for your banker? Here are seven strategies to get a loan approved for your start-up business.

1. Recognize the fact that a loan approval for a start-up business is more difficult to obtain and will require more time and patience on your part. Many banks will not even consider a loan request for a start-up.
2. Do not rush the application process. Let the banker set the pace for loan approval.
3. Supply whatever additional items that are sure to be requested. You can increase your odds for loan approval by helping your banker become more comfortable with the risks associated with the loan request.
4. Emphasize your experience in your field of work. You can never do too much of this.
5. Discuss the liquidity of your collateral package. If a supplier offers 100% buy back of inventory, be sure your

banker knows this fact.

6. Show that you have equity in the transaction. Tell your banker how much money you have invested in the business and specifically how it was applied.
7. Prepare a reliable budget and carefully list the assumptions you used to build it.

Specific Strategy # 10

Have plenty of patience if you are applying for a start-up business loan.

" Never rush the bank "
for a credit decision. It usually
works against you.

" Life is too short for you "
to accomplish your goals
without the help of others.

CHAPTER 20

I DON'T LOOK THAT OLD... BUT I DO HAVE THAT MUCH EXPERIENCE

Let's say that you want to borrow money to open a retail jewelry store. One of your banker's primary concerns is to assess the amount of experience you have in the operation of retail jewelry.

Highlight your experience in this line of work as much as possible. A personal resume, including detailed biographical information, is a must. If you recently worked for a similar company and decided to strike out on your own, then your position is one of strength, particularly if you had worked yourself into a management position with your previous employer. Note specific problems that might have occurred with that previous employer and how you played an integral part in resolving them in a satisfactory manner. You want to show that you have firing-line experience in your field of work. If you were actually involved in determining the solution to past problems, then explain the thought processes you went through in actually coming to your conclusions. This kind of information is important to your banker. Include it as a written narrative when you submit your loan package to your banker.

Also, be sure to emphasize the years of experience of your employees. What are the total years of experience for your entire staff? What special courses or seminars have you and your staff attended? Better yet, have you ever taught or lectured on your core business at any trade schools or associations?

Maybe your parents started the business and you have been involved in it since childhood. Will you continue to operate it in the same manner, or do you have plans to take it to a new plateau? Or maybe you are taking over the family business after having been in some other field for a long time. How will your experiences add to this venture?

Remember to draw from your experiences! Share them all with your banker.

If you are acquiring or doing a start-up of a business in which you have same-industry experience, then you are at an obvious advantage. If you are entering an industry in which you have no experience, it is important to discuss the similarities. Business issues relating to finance, personnel, sales, marketing, administration, etc. are basically the same in all industries. The only difference is the product or service that is being delivered.

Focus on the big picture with your banker. Be sure to emphasize your general ability and experience, and how it qualifies you to effectively operate your business.

> **Specific Strategy # 11**
>
> **❝ You should constantly emphasize your business experience. ❞**

❝ No amount of computer **❞**
technology will ever replace
the personal contact required
between a business owner
and his banker.

❝ A friend once told me that **❞**
the bravest person in the world
is the small business owner.

CHAPTER 21

I Need To See Something In XXL

Pick a bank that offers products and services that are compatible to your needs. In the last few years, many banks have realized they cannot be everything to everybody. Consequently, many smaller banks are identifying their special areas of expertise.

"Boutique" banks, as they are often called, may specialize in catering to import/export business, small business or high net worth individuals. Some banks, exclusively owned and operated by women, offer special benefits to women business owners. There are many minority-owned banks which cater to customers with similar interests and backgrounds.

Look at what your bank has to offer to you. Let's say you run your own business and need access to an operating line of credit. Make sure your bank offers such a service. Do you require receivable financing? Saturday banking? Extended drive-in hours? My bank keeps its drive-in windows open until 8:00 p.m., and our customers love it.

How important is responsiveness to you? Will you need quick answers to your loan requests? Ask your banker about her personal lending limit. What is the lending limit for management? What is the legal limit for the bank? Will that limit meet your needs? What is the turnaround time for a loan request that must go to the board of directors?

Usually, the larger the bank, the longer it will take to receive a response to your loan request. A larger bank, with several layers of management, tends to be more bureaucratic. A smaller bank may be able to approve your request much faster. One disadvantage with the smaller bank, however, is that its loan limit will be much lower than a larger bank. Make sure the legal limit for your bank is well in excess of your borrowing needs. Prepare a list of your financial needs and refer to it when you interview your banker.

Specific Strategy # 12

Make a list of the financial needs you will require from your bank.

CHAPTER 22

WHATEVER!

There are eight operating principles you should expect from the staff at your bank. Discuss these expectations early on with your banker. When you mention these standards, it's a signal that not only do you expect them from bank employees, but at your own place of business as well. They are:

1. Reliability
2. Appreciation
3. Accuracy
4. Knowledge
5. Efficiency
6. Responsiveness
7. Accessibility
8. Respect

Whenever these operating principles are firmly in place at your bank, you will never feel that you are being treated like a number. You will feel like a customer whose business is appreciated. It's easy to "talk" quality customer service, but putting it into daily practice is another thing indeed. Quality customer service requires constant training and managing of people. Talk to your banker about how you work hard to deliver quality customer service to your customers, and how you expect it from your bank as well.

Specific Strategy # 13

Make sure your banker knows that you understand and expect quality customer service.

The 1-800 Sales Representative

I dialed the toll-free number to open a mutual fund account over the telephone. The sales representative who answered my call had the most "stand-up" voice I had ever heard. Her tone was assertive, and her style was straightforward with no hesitations. As she began gathering information from me, I began to register the impression of a successful professional person. For all I knew, the call could have been taken in the midst of a crowded cubicle environment, yet I envisioned someone ensconced on the top floor of a high rise office building who literally stood up to take the call.

The sales representative closed by encouraging me to record the date, time, her name and my transaction number. Her sales skills made me feel comfortable in sending my money to someone I had never met and to someplace I had never been.

What a sales culture!

Recruit the right people! Train them. Retain them!

Summary

Strategy # 8

Have passion and commitment for what you do.

Strategy # 9

Don't pick a bank, pick a banker.

Strategy # 10

Have plenty of patience if you are applying for a start-up business loan.

Strategy # 11

You should constantly emphasize your business experience.

Strategy # 12

Make a list of the financial needs you will require from your bank.

Strategy # 13

Make sure your banker knows that you understand and expect quality customer service.

CHAPTER 23

TURN THE LIGHTS DOWN, I'M COMING RIGHT OVER

A mistake that most people make is to call their banker only when they need to borrow money. You should have much more frequent contact with your banker.

Call and visit on a regular basis to discuss something other than borrowing money. When you are making an appointment for such a meeting, be sure to tell the loan officer that you don't need to borrow money, but need advice on some other matter. This immediately puts the loan officer in a more relaxed frame of mind. Otherwise, throughout your visit, your banker will be thinking, "When is he going to ask for money and how much will it be?" Communication will not be as effective and you will not have a successful meeting.

Making credit decisions creates stress for many loan officers. Having to say "NO" to a credit request really places a burden on a loan officer's shoulders. You cannot imagine how heavy that phone gets when it is necessary to call an applicant and explain why his or her credit request was denied.

Help your banker to feel more comfortable and relaxed with you. Put him at ease before you ever arrive for your appointment. The results will be a more receptive banker who can suggest ways to structure a loan to reach your goals. Develop the aura of a give-and-take session as opposed to a question and answer period, and you have set the stage for a very productive meeting where the two of you may seem to back into the idea that a loan might be the very answer to your needs. This way, you have actually allowed your banker to suggest that you need a loan, as opposed to you coming in and asking for it. Your banker will now feel more of a responsibility to get the loan approved, because, after all, it was his idea.

Specific Strategy # 14

You should schedule occasional visits with your banker when you don't need to borrow money.

CHAPTER 24

Please Go With Me!

When you go for that first official appointment to make a loan request, be prepared - mentally prepared. Don't take papers, statements, or tax returns. The purpose of this initial meeting is for you to get to know your banker. You first talk about your business, then ask the banker to tell you briefly about himself and the bank. This meeting should last less than one hour.

If you have a spouse who works with you, an office manager, or another person who is important in your daily business operation, take them with you to the bank. This is a sign that you have established depth of management in your company. Your banker will probably feel that you are less likely to stretch the truth with others present, and it also provides a good learning experience for anyone who accompanies you. Your first visit usually does not disclose sensitive issues meant only for company shareholders' ears. When you include a key employee in the initial loan request meeting, it serves as a good faith signal that there are no deep, dark secrets about company operations.

If you were referred to the bank by a friend, then certainly take that person with you for the introductory visit. A banker definitely prefers a referral from a good customer rather than a "walk-in." Walk-ins are usually people who got so mad at their last bank over a service charge or a loan denial that they left in a rage in search of greener pastures. Even if your last banking experience was similar to this, remember to position yourself now in a positive manner. Be a referral - not a walk-in. Take your friend with you. It makes a big difference.

Specific Strategy # 15

Have an introductory visit with your banker before you apply for your loan.

CHAPTER 25

NEED IT BY 5 ... I GOTTA MAKE PAYROLL

If you rush into the bank for a loan half-cocked and ill-prepared, you will only convince your banker that you're a poor planner with little foresight. Don't let this happen to you.

Bankers become very suspicious when pushy borrowers attempt to create a sense of urgency. The wagons start to circle when this happens. A loan decision is not made until all the facts are gathered, and a rush decision does not allow time for this fact-finding mission. The banker wants to avoid any situation where negative facts arise after the loan has been made. Remember that bankers are very conservative and normally slow decision makers. You will not be successful in rushing a credit decision with an experienced banker.

Don't put your loan officer on the spot by demanding an immediate answer to your loan request. Allow him the time to review your application and get back with you. If you push too hard, the response probably will be, "Well, if you need an answer now, the answer is no. But if you can give me a little time to work on your request, I will be glad to try and get it approved."

The only time you will be successful in rushing a credit decision is after you have developed a solid, long-lasting relationship with your banker. Once you have done this, you will have all the necessary ingredients in hand for a quick loan approval.

Specific Strategy # 16

Never rush your banker for a credit decision.

CHAPTER 26

HEY GUYS! PLEASE DON'T EAT AT YOUR DESK TODAY

My first meeting with a new customer is usually held in my bank office. We discuss the nature of their business and the reasons for their loan request. I then provide a list of information that should be included in the loan package.

For the second meeting, I prefer to visit the customer's place of business. This gives me an opportunity to tour their offices and to pick up the completed loan application package.

So, invite your banker to visit you. This meeting will be very valuable in acquainting him with your business. The more familiar your banker is with you and your business, the more he will be able to help you. He also will become much more comfortable with you and your management abilities after visiting you in your own environment.

It's a good idea for bankers to get out and visit the location of any business during the loan underwriting process. Some may not make the time to do this. Insist that your banker visit your business before the credit decision is made.

Here are some tips to influence the loan decision in your favor prior to a banker's visit. Don't invite your banker during lunch when many of your employees will be away from their work stations. Schedule the meeting during your busiest time so he sees a high level of activity. See that the facilities are very clean inside and outside, including the parking lot, hallways, kitchen, bathrooms, etc. This attention to detail is important and will be duly noted, I assure you.

Brief your employees that your banker is coming for a visit, and ask that they be sure to put their best foot forward. Explain that the visit is very important to you, to the business, and to them!

You want the loan officer to be able to return to his loan committee and say, "I have visited this company and it is very neat and clean. It appears to be well managed and I found all of the employees to be very warm and friendly."

It is critical that your banker leaves the company visit with a favorable impression.

Specific Strategy # 17

**Invite your banker
to your place of business.**

CHAPTER 27

ALL RIGHT, IT'S SHOW TIME!

When your banker visits your business, be sure to involve your employees. It is impossible to deliver quality customer service without quality employees. You represent a better risk to the bank if you have assembled a staff that is friendly, bright and assertive. Showcase your people. Demonstrate to the banker that you have surrounded yourself with smart people who are career-oriented.

A bank is only as good as its bankers. The same holds true for your business. Your company is only as good as the people who work for you. If you have excellent skills in managing your employees, provide examples of what you have done. If managing the employees has been delegated to a junior person in the company, then highlight their abilities and experience. Your banker will be looking for depth in management, so involve your middle managers in the visit so he can get a good feel for their abilities. If you have good quality people, then make sure your banker knows how strongly you feel about them.

Offer some examples of how you have improved morale in your company, or how you have set up a training program to improve the sales culture. This is the kind of information you need to share during a visit with your banker.

Specific Strategy # 18

Introduce your banker to your key employees.

I Think I'm Beginning To Understand

Here's a story I frequently share with my staff:

"We are a team, and everyone's job is equally important. Let's say a customer walks into the lobby of the bank, sits down at your desk and reorders checks. Two weeks later, he still doesn't have his checks. He calls in to complain. His checks finally arrive two days later, but his name is misspelled.

When that customer needs to borrow $200,000 for his business, do you think he will trust us to handle the loan when we couldn't even get his name spelled right on his checks?

Never underestimate the importance of your job."

" *I Said*, I Need It By 5! I Gotta Make Payroll! "

CHAPTER 28

AM I IN THE RIGHT PLACE?

If you don't already enjoy a solid relationship with a banker, then go through this exercise. Visit all of the banks in your area. Just walk into the lobby of each office and wander around. When approached, ask for some new account information. Listen carefully and be observant. Politely thank them for their time and leave. What did you learn?

As you approached the building, did you notice if the parking lot was clean, or was it littered with cigarette butts and other trash? Was the grass neatly mowed, shrubs and flower beds attractively trimmed? When you entered, was the building clean? How about the doors and windows, the carpets?

Your impressions of the employees: were they well dressed and professional in appearance? What about the sales culture? Did the customer service representative seem eager to share information with you, or acted too busy to give you personal attention?

When you left, did you feel they really wanted your business? Did they ask for your name and phone number to follow up with you later? Did they ask for your business?

The answers to these questions will tell you a lot about the personality of the bank. From these simple observations, you can assess the bank's attention to detail, sales culture, level of in-house training and aggressiveness for new business. All of these things are important to you.

If you are going to borrow your money from this bank, and deposit your hard-earned pay check in this bank, then make sure attention to detail is a number one priority. If they cannot even clean up the floor in the foyer, then I certainly would not trust them to clean up a problem with an automatic insurance draft.

You want a bank that is spit-shined on the inside and the outside. Expect well-dressed and very informative sales people. Look for assertive and knowledgeable bankers who know their products well and speak with confidence in describing them. Pay attention to your local newspapers. See which banks are advertising and what services they provide. Make sure that the banker you pick is working for a bank that has products and services that are compatible with your needs.

How can you find out which bank is best for you? Ask! When you visit each bank, simply ask for an average customer profile. Also, when you read the newspaper, don't just look at the paid ads. Look at the human interest stories about local banks. Study local news sections and social sections to see which banks are active in these areas. These items will tell you a lot about the personality of the bank and its bankers. You want to be exactly the type of customer this bank is seeking.

Specific Strategy # 19

Be a target customer for your bank.

SUMMARY

Strategy # 14

You should schedule occasional visits with your banker when you don't need to borrow money.

Strategy # 15

Have an introductory visit with your banker before you apply for your loan.

Strategy # 16

Never rush your banker for a credit decision.

Strategy # 17

Invite your banker to your place of business.

Strategy # 18

Introduce your banker to your key employees.

Strategy # 19

Be a target customer for your bank.

CHAPTER 29

SHOW ME YOURS, I'LL SHOW YOU MINE

Ever seen your credit report? Know what it contains and make it work in your favor. I have seen a poor credit report ruin the chances of loan approval when all other criteria met the grade. There are many things you can do to avoid this potential trap.

First and foremost, call your bank to see which credit reporting agency they use. There are many agencies that are available to financial institutions. Your bank has probably singled out one for exclusive use. Next, call that credit agency and request a copy of your report. Be sure to ask for reports in different variations of your name. For example, if your name is James Stephen Anderson, also ask for files in J. Stephen, James S. and J.S. All of these names should report under your social security number, but don't count on it.

When you receive the report, check your name, address and social security number to make sure it is correct. Review the list of creditors on your report to make sure it is accurate. It is not uncommon for accounts to be listed on your report that do not belong to you. You would be unnecessarily penalized when your banker compares your income against the debts listed on your report if some of the debts listed are not actually yours.

Is the payment history accurate? If you have never been late in payments, this should be reflected. If you have had some late payments, are those late payments accurately reported?

Call your credit bureau to find out the procedure for making corrections to your report. There undoubtedly will be changes, and these can take several weeks to be reflected in your revised report. Keep documented evidence of these changes and include them with your loan package when you submit it to the bank.

If there is any information in the file that requires an explanation, then write a "consumer statement" and ask that it be a part of your credit report.

Call your banker and say, "I just got a copy of my credit report. Will you explain it to me and see if there is anything I need to do?" Your banker should be very willing to give you this advice.

Specific Strategy # 20

Know what is on your credit bureau report.

CHAPTER
30

IF BORROWING MONEY IS SO EASY, WHY IS MY LIFE SO DIFFICULT?

How many inquiries do you have on your credit report? Whenever you approach anyone for credit - a bank, a department store, a landlord, an auto dealer - they will all make an inquiry through a credit reporting agency to review your credit history. Every time this happens, an inquiry is recorded on your credit report. Consequently, if you have applied to several banks for the same loan request, many inquiries will appear on your credit report. It will show who called in for a copy, as well as the date of inquiry. This represents a red flag to your banker. Bankers become very suspicious when they see a lot of recent inquiries on your credit report. It makes it appear that you have been feverishly trying to obtain a loan, but have been turned down by every lender.

If you are shopping around for an automobile or a new apartment, do not, I repeat, do not let them run a credit report on you until you have decided that you are ready to do business with them. Creditors are not allowed to pull your credit report unless you give them written approval, usually through some form of application. If you allow an auto dealer to run a credit report on you when you know that you are not interested in the car, then you have allowed an unnecessary inquiry to be made in your file. When your banker pulls your credit report and sees ten different inquiries within the last week, he will not take your application very seriously.

Specific Strategy # 21

Do everything you can to control the number of inquiries made to your credit bureau file.

THE BANK CARRIED ME LONGER THAN MOMMA DID

Review the account payment history on the accounts on your credit report to make sure it is accurate. For example, if it erroneously reports you have paid two payments over thirty days late on your mortgage when in fact you have never been late, then you must immediately get busy to correct the mistake. You will need to contact the creditor who reported the incorrect information and instruct them to transmit that correction to the credit agency. This can be time-consuming, but you must do it. If you have perfect credit, then you certainly want your credit report to reflect it.

What if you don't have perfect credit? If you have had some late payments with your creditors in the past, you want to make sure your banker understands the specific circumstances that created the situation. It is best for you if all of your late payments occurred in one specific period of time. This makes it easier to understand that you hit a financially troubled time, perhaps due to divorce, serious illness or loss of job, but are now maintaining a good payment record. If, however, your banker sees a pattern of late payments through the years with different creditors, then you may have just run out of excuses. If you have had a significant number of late payments, or worse, liens, judgments or a possible bankruptcy, then some specific strategies are in order.

The credit agency will allow you to add a consumer statement to your report to serve as an explanation to any creditor who pulls your report. If you have had some credit problems, then you should definitely take advantage of the consumer statement in order to help explain your circumstances. In addition to the consumer statement, you should write a detailed letter surrounding your credit problems and include it with your loan application. If you have previously filed a bankruptcy, be sure to ask if your bank's lending policy will allow you to qualify for a loan and if so, what conditions are available.

If you have had significant credit problems, then it is unlikely that you will be able to borrow unless you are willing to put up cash collateral or bring in a cosigner who is satisfactory to the bank. For whatever the reason, you must admit that you have had credit problems and that you do represent a higher risk to the bank because of this. Bad credit will not allow you as much flexibility to pick the banker of your choice.

Banks have different policies regarding how they underwrite loan requests for applicants with poor credit. For example, at my bank we almost never approve a loan request for someone who has previously filed bankruptcy. Regardless of the degree of credit problems, be sure to warn your banker and tell him that you will provide detailed explanations when you make application. Make sure he hears about your credit problems directly from you. Don't let him be surprised when he reviews your credit report. If you fail to discuss any credit problems early on, then you could be wasting your time and your banker's as well.

Specific Strategy # 22

Explain a credit problem to your banker before he finds out about it on his own.

" The bank helped me out… " of my house.

" Treat me like a number and I'll put sardines in my safe deposit box. "

CHAPTER 32

I NEED A LOAN, NOT A LECTURE

Too many people do not understand how important it is to have a good credit history. If you have recently applied for a mortgage loan, you know what a hassle even one late payment on an account can create. A late payment can set off a campaign of time-consuming letter writing to explain the circumstances for the late payment.

Don't get lazy and miss a bill payment date. It will cost you a lot of time and energy later on to explain why you made a late payment during a time of no particular financial hardship.

Bankers love loan applicants with "clean" credit. A "clean" credit report is one that shows several creditors with no late payments at all. It is my experience that most people always have at least one issue on their credit report that requires further explanation. If you are one of the few who indeed have perfect credit, then make a big deal about it. Say to your banker, "I understand how important it is to have good credit. I always pay my bills on time, no matter what."

Be sure to tell your banker about your good credit as soon as possible in your initial conversations. By telling your banker how good your credit is and how hard you work to keep it that way, you put him in a very comfortable mode. He doesn't have to worry about a credit "surprise" at a later time. He is able to focus on best structuring your credit needs.

A clean credit report tells a banker a lot about your character. We all have a tough time keeping the bills paid on time, regardless of our income level. Bankers realize that people with clean credit reports are fiscally responsible and treat their creditors with respect.

Specific Strategy # 23

If you have "perfect" credit, always be sure to emphasize it early in the conversation with your banker.

CHAPTER 33

MY CAR GOT REPOSSESSED... I'M ON MY FEET AGAIN

Your payment is due at the bank. You don't have the money. What do you do? Turn off your phones? Change your name? It might work for a while, but you would never be able to borrow money again.

Most people practice avoidance when they can't pay on time. They do this by not returning phone calls or not signing for registered mail. They avoid their banker at a time when their banker could probably help them the most.

Not being able to pay on time should not be an embarrassing situation for you. It happens to everyone at some time or another. So what do you do?

Here are three suggestions:
1. Call your loan officer and tell him you will be late.
2. Tell him when you will make a payment and how much you will pay.
3. Keep your promise.

Possible replies from your banker? Here are a few:
1. That will be fine, as long as you keep your promise.
2. For a small extension fee, you can skip this month's payment completely.
3. Maybe we need to restructure all of your debts and lower your total monthly payments.

Handle your payment problems in a businesslike manner. Discuss the problem with your banker. He will respect you for it and it may even enhance your chances of approval for your next loan request.

Specific Strategy # 24

Always call your banker before your payment becomes past due.

TRICK OR TREAT

He owed me $10,000 and he was past due over ninety days. He would not respond to my letters or return my phone calls. I went by his condo twice but he wouldn't answer the door.

On Halloween night, dressed in my favorite "Farmer Jones" outfit, I rang his doorbell. "Trick or treat!" I said as he opened the door. That was a Kodak moment.

SUMMARY

Strategy # 20

Know what is on your credit bureau report.

Strategy # 21

Do everything you can to control the number of inquiries made to your credit bureau file.

Strategy # 22

Explain a credit problem to your banker before he finds out about it on his own.

Strategy # 23

If you have "perfect" credit always be sure to emphasize it early in the conversation with your banker.

Strategy # 24

Always call your banker before your payment becomes past due.

CHAPTER 34

Don't Laugh... I Really Owe This Much

One thing that delays the approval of your loan request is an incomplete or inaccurate personal financial statement. You definitely will build credibility with your banker by submitting an accurate and conservative personal financial statement. An error-free statement will save time for you and your banker, and assures a faster response to your loan request.

Make sure your statement balances. So many people provide personal financial statements where the numbers simply don't add up. This may seem routine, but problems will persist if you don't get the numbers right.

Give your banker the original statement, typed, signed and dated. Keep a copy in your files. When you have to provide an updated statement each year, you'll simplify the process by making changes to your filed copy, rather than starting at ground zero.

Be sure to give accurate information on your statement. A common mistake is to overstate the value of assets. Do not overstate this figure simply to increase your personal net worth.

If your personal residence is worth $100,000, then don't try to fudge and list it at $150,000 merely to inflate your total assets. The truth will come out. Your banker may very well be familiar with the market values for your neighborhood and will immediately question the $150,000 figure. Or if you are pledging a second mortgage against your home, an appraisal will be ordered that will provide an accurate value statement. Do not waste time during a loan application process by inflating asset values. Conservative values on the asset side of your personal financial statement will build more credibility with your banker than artificial net worth.

Don't under estimate or completely forget about some of your liabilities. Upon receiving your signed credit application, the first thing your banker will do is pull a credit report. The information obtained from the credit bureau will reflect virtually all of your debts. It will include the names of your creditors, the original and current balances and your payment history. Your banker will compare the debt you report on your personal financial statement to the debts that are reported on your credit bureau report. If there are debts on the credit report which you did not list on your personal financial statement, then you have set the stage for an awkward situation. Don't let it appear that you were trying to "hide" any of your debts. Be honest. With thorough, accurate information, your banker may suggest a total restructuring of debts to make your life easier.

If you own your own company, give special consideration to how you report its value on your personal financial statement. If your company is closely-held, and especially if you are the sole shareholder, your banker will have a tendency to deduct the company value from your personal financial statement to determine your true net worth. Consult your CPA or an industry consultant on how to best reflect the value of your company. For the benefit of your banker, be sure to footnote your method of valuation somewhere on your personal financial statement.

You can build significant credibility with your banker early in the loan approval process by submitting a conservative and accurate personal financial statement.

Specific Strategy # 25

Always submit an honest and accurate personal financial statement.

"Trick or Treat, Smell My Feet. Pay Me Now Or Be Dead Meat!"

CHAPTER 35

DOES MINE LOOK PITIFUL?

The successful operation of your business depends in a large part on how well you understand your financial statements, so be prepared to discuss them with your banker. Your banker will be asking you many questions about your statements, so you want to be very knowledgeable. They are your statements, so if anyone should understand them, you should.

Your understanding of your financial statements begins with your relationship with your accountant. You pay good money for an accountant's services, and you should feel comfortable in asking any question, no matter how silly it may seem.

You are the expert when it comes to what is happening in your office, or the warehouse, or on the road. You are in control. You know everything that is happening in the company. You know who you owe and who you don't owe. You know who is behind with you and who your biggest customers are. But do you know how all of this reflects on your balance sheet and your P & L (profit and loss) statement? With just a couple of simple questions, your banker can detect how well you understand your statements. So, what should you do if you don't know how to read your financial statements?

Ask your accountant to explain your statements to you. Don't act like you understand each point, unless you do. If your accountant will not take the time to explain your statements, then change accountants or, if you don't understand the explanations supplied, change accountants.

Too many borrowers or would-be borrowers consider their financial statements to be a nuisance. I can recall many times when I have requested current financial statements from an applicant only to have the applicant pick up the phone and instruct their accountant to send current financial statements directly to the bank.

Don't do that. You should have a draft of the financials sent directly to you. After reviewing them for accuracy, you can release copies to the bank. At the same time, use these statements as a powerful management tool by comparing them to prior periods. Proper review of your financial statements will help you run a successful business.

Specific Strategy # 26

Make sure you understand your financial statements well enough to discuss them with your banker.

CHAPTER 36

BY THE NUMBERS, PLEASE

Bankers always become suspicious when borrowers or applicants refuse to furnish financial statements on time. You must be hiding something. The company must not be profitable. Sales must be way down. Or maybe you're just not having statements prepared regularly, which is also a miscue by management.

You should submit financial statements on a timely basis to avoid any unnecessary suspicions by your banker. Find out if your banker needs your company financial statements on a monthly, quarterly or semiannual basis. Send a letter to your accountant with instructions to send copies of your financials directly to the bank after you have reviewed them. Send a copy of that letter to your banker.

Your banker then knows that you not only understand when company financial statements are due, but you have gone one step further and instructed your accountant to send them to the bank. That letter will be placed in your loan file. If future statements are not received on a timely basis, the bank will call your accountant. They won't be bugging you.

If you will have your company financial statements sent to the attention of your loan officer before he asks for them, you will become one of his most popular customers.

If you want to be his favorite customer, then call him and say, "I just received my quarterly financials and would like to make an appointment so that we can review them together." Any banker would love to hear these words.

Specific Strategy # 27

Send your financial statements to the bank on a timely basis.

CHAPTER 37

I Don't Need To Stop And Ask Directions

I have seen many business owners pay thousands of dollars to a consultant to write a business plan for their company. The theory seems to be that if this business plan comes in two volumes and weighs at least eight pounds, then it must be a good one. So then what happens to it? It usually goes on the bookshelf and begins to collect dust. But hey, you have a business plan, don't you? No, you don't.

A business plan is a living, breathing document that can be a valuable management tool. Simply put, it spells out where you are going and how you plan to get there. At our bank, our business plan has twelve short chapters. The average chapter is only three pages. Each chapter addresses a strategic area of the bank, i.e., asset quality, working capital, merger and acquisitions. At each monthly board meeting, we review one of the twelve chapters for revisions. Consequently, our business plan is constantly being updated and no chapter ever goes more than one year without being reviewed. I refer to my business plan constantly as I manage the bank.

You say your company is too small for a business plan? Never. I hear business owners say, "That's silly, I know what my plans are." Maybe you do, but how do others know? Your spouse, your banker, your employees, your suppliers, your CPA - how do they know? These people can serve you well if you share your vision with them.

There is no right way or wrong way to write a business plan. Simply identify where you want to take your company within the next three to five years in total sales, net income, number of locations, etc. Identify the resources you will need to make it happen. Keep your plan brief and to the point. It should be written so that in your absence, someone else can read it, understand it, and step into your shoes to perform exactly what needs to be done.

Your banker will ask if you have a business plan. Having one, and using it on a consistent basis, will help convince your banker that you are a good planner with considerable foresight.

Specific Strategy # 28

You must have a reliable written business plan.

CHAPTER 38

I'VE NEVER PROPOSED TO ANYONE BEFORE

"How much money do you need to borrow?" I asked. "Well, I really don't know," he replied. I thought to myself, "Come back when you figure it out and don't waste my time!"

This happens all the time. I see business owners operating from the seat of their pants, with no real focus on their business.

If you are getting ready to borrow some money from the bank, you must have a "Written Loan Proposal." What is this written loan proposal? It is simply a letter you write to your banker outlining the basic information about your loan request.

Your loan proposal should include the following information:

1. A list of the names of all borrowers, including addresses, social security numbers and phone numbers.
2. The requested loan amount.

3. The purpose of the loan, as well as how its proceeds will be spent.
4. A company history and a profile of its operations.
5. Resumes on yourself and any key employees.
6. A clear identification of your product or service.
7. An analysis of your company's strengths and weaknesses in comparison to your competition.
8. A target customer profile, with an explanation of why your target customer does business with you.
9. A list of all the collateral available to secure the loan.
10. A personal financial statement on all the principals and interim financial statements for the business.
11. The last three years' tax returns on all the principals, as well as the business.

Go into your banker's office with a written loan proposal that includes all of this information and you have significantly sped up the loan decision process. You have shown that you have spent some careful and deliberate time considering this loan request.

Specific Strategy # 29

Always take the time to prepare a "Written Loan Proposal."

Sometimes It Just Don't Add Up

A reliable budget is a valuable management tool for any business owner. Unfortunately, most small business owners never prepare a budget until their banker asks for it. That's too bad because a budget is a management tool that should be studied at the end of each month. Otherwise, how do you know if you are on track?

Budgets that are prepared at the last minute to be included in a loan package tend not to be accurate. It seems these budgets are "shaped" to help facilitate a loan approval.

The two most common mistakes are:

1. Total sales are overestimated. If your budget calls for a 50% annual increase in sales, then you must qualify this increase with your assumptions. Exactly how do you plan to increase sales to this level? You will lose credibility with your banker if you cannot justify your sales projections.

2. Total expenses are underestimated. Somehow expenses always exceed projections. Family budgets, business budgets, building a new home . . . whatever we do, it seems we always spend more than we think we will. Remember to allow yourself plenty of contingency funds in the expense section of your budget.

Prepare a reliable working budget. At the end of the year, your banker will compare your year-end financials to the budget you previously furnished. You want these reports to be very close or you will lose credibility.

The last thing you want to happen is to go to the bank two months after you close your "big" loan and say, "I need some more money."

If I were your banker, I would ask, "Really, why is that?" When you would reply, "Well, my sales just didn't get to where I thought they would" or "Well, some unexpected expenses just killed me," I would sigh and say, "Well, let's take a look at the budget you gave me and see exactly what happened."

If you prepare a realistic budget, then find that you are not happy with the bottom line income, ask your banker to help you figure out how to reach your goals.

Specific Strategy # 30

Always prepare a realistic budget.

THIS LITTLE PIGGY HAD A PLAN

You can have the best product in the world, but unless the world knows about it, you will never sell a unit.

I feel strongly about my bank. I think if everyone in my primary market area were to come into my bank and meet my staff, they would immediately fall in love with us and move all their loans and deposits to our facility.

Do your feelings about your company translate into action? Do you have a marketing plan? How do you market to your target customers? Who are your target customers?

You might think that last question sounds silly, but our bank was seven years old before we defined our target customer. Prior to that, we tried to accomodate everyone. It was a case of everything for everybody, anyone who walked in the door.

Amazing things happened after we defined our target customer. Our personnel changed, and we became very focused. Attitudes improved. Net income went up. We grew by 50% in six months.

All of this happened because we wrote a marketing plan to identify our target customer and steps to draw him to our facility.

This simple three-page plan outlines such strategies as:

1. Assigned sales calls
2. Effective referral programs
3. Power networking strategies
4. Newspaper ads
5. Free customer seminars
6. Employee incentive programs
7. Business development committee

Put your plans for raising customer awareness into writing, and see your ideas come to life.

Specific Strategy # 31

**Write a short,
easy-to-understand marketing plan.**

SUMMARY

Strategy # 25

Always submit an honest and accurate personal financial statement.

Strategy # 26

Make sure you understand your financial statements well enough to discuss them with your banker.

Strategy # 27

Send your financial statements to the bank on a timely basis.

Strategy # 28

You must have a reliable written business plan.

Strategy # 29

Always take the time to prepare a "Written Loan Proposal."

Strategy # 30

Always prepare a realistic budget.

Strategy # 31

Write a short, easy-to-understand marketing plan.

" This Little Piggy Had A Plan. "

CHAPTER 41

No, Not Yet, I Said

Never try to negotiate interest rates or closing costs for your loan during the application stage. Wait until after your loan has been approved, and then you can negotiate from a position of strength.

During the application phase, your banker is reviewing all the information to determine whether this is a loan he wants to make. He may have to be very competitive with terms and conditions in order to win your business. You do not have to convince him what a good customer you will be. He already figured that out himself after he studied your financial statements.

So, when your banker finally calls and says that your loan request has been approved, you are ready to discuss pricing. Until this point you have talked in general terms. Now you can begin to negotiate interest rates, points and closing costs, but not to a fault.

If you are a shrewd businessperson, your banker will expect you to try and cut the best deal you can for yourself. Wait until after your loan is approved before you negotiate. If you offer ultimatums at the onset, your loan may be denied based on that reason. Never let this happen to you. Let the loan get approved first. You want your banker to invest the time and energy required in getting the loan approved. By that time he feels a sense of ownership. After he has received loan approval he will want to close your loan as quickly as possible to help meet his personal production goals. At this point, you are better positioned to negotiate terms and conditions.

Too many times, somebody will call me on the phone, and their first question is, "What will the interest rate be?" It's hard to really answer that question because it depends on a lot of circumstances. Are you already a customer of the bank? Do you have other loans with the bank? Will you keep your deposits at the bank and if so, how much? What kind of collateral are you offering? As you can see, it is premature to try and set the interest rate on a loan until all information is gathered. Negotiate from a position of strength - wait until your loan is approved.

Specific Strategy # 32

Negotiate terms and conditions after you get loan approval.

CHAPTER 42

IF BORROWING MONEY IS SUCH A PAIN, WHY DO I FEEL SO GOOD?

A good relationship with your banker is a lot like a successful marriage. Both require some work, because you will eventually encounter troublesome times. Don't overreact and say things you may later regret.

An example: a very good borrower of mine approached me about lending him money to build homes in a new developing subdivision. After gathering all the necessary information on the transaction, I visited the site. When I got to the development entrance, I detected a "foul" odor in the air - two active poultry houses located across the street. I met the borrower in his sales office and reviewed his site plan. On the way back to the office, I decided that every aspect of the project looked good, but the odor from the poultry houses would certainly be a turn-off to a potential buyer. I decided to deny the loan request for that reason. I discussed my concern with the borrower and he seemed to take the news very well. No ranting, no raving, no excuses.

Listen to how the borrower followed up in the next few days. His response was well planned and presented in a very businesslike manner. He had gone to the local property tax office and paid $2 a piece for aerial photographs of neighboring subdivisions developed within the last two years. He had carefully highlighted the poultry houses on these maps to show their proximity to certain subdivisions. He presented overwhelming evidence that the poultry houses apparently had no effect on the sale of homes in several successful subdivisions. I offered this new information to my Directors Loan Committee and the project was approved.

The point is that the borrower did not become angry when originally denied his loan requests. He followed up with information to further back his original request. I have seen many borrowers over the years taking a different tactic, becoming angry, storming out of the bank, only to start the process all over again with a new relationship with a new banker.

If your loan request is denied, then listen very carefully to the reasons behind it. Go back and regroup. Figure out a way that you can satisfy the banker's concerns and present yourself as less of a risk to the bank.

If you have chosen the right banker, then he will do his

best to help you find ways to get it approved. Remember, it's his job to find ways to lend money, not ways to deny requests. When your banker tells you "no," make sure he specifically tells you the reasons behind the decision. Ask for advice on how any concerns can be addressed. Get your banker to help you, but know that you have the ultimate responsibility. Get the creative juices flowing and handle your situation the same way my poultry house borrower did. He controlled his own destiny. The manner in which he handled that situation certainly strengthened his position with his banker. He had an opportunity to burn a bridge with his banker, but rather he strengthened it through his actions.

Specific Strategy # 33

**Don't over react if you
are turned down on a loan request.**

" I Bet They'll Return My Phone Calls Now! "

DO WHAT I SAY, NOT WHAT I DO

It's my personal observation as a banker that people usually call to see me only when they need to borrow money. Don't fall into that trap.

You may only have loan needs every two or three years. Don't wait until then to talk with your banker. Consider a call when you want financial advice or counseling. Bankers now feel more responsibility to share their experience and advice with customers. When economic problems develop, as they have over the last few years, bankers can look back and see how more assertive counseling on their part may have saved a borrower from getting into trouble, or even losing a business. If you have a banker who is still unwilling to share his experience with you, then maybe you have picked the wrong banker. If you have a banker who has not been in the business long enough to have any experience, then you have certainly chosen the wrong banker.

My best loan relationships are with borrowers who keep me informed of what is happening in their companies. Some of these borrowers will come in two or three times a year, and we will sit together to review their financial statements. We will study the balance sheet and discuss the mix of assets and liabilities. We analyze changes since last year and any possible developing trends. We take a close look at the profit and loss statement, looking at every expense item and reviewing it on a percentage basis as it relates to total sales. This is the only way you can find out if overhead and operating costs are staying in line. Your banker should be able to provide you with average industry ratios for your size company.

While you may feel very confident about your ability to run your company, you must admit that life is like a classroom. We will never learn everything there is to know about our respective businesses. A know-it-all approach does not appeal to your banker. Ask for his input. Take his advice, the advice you receive from others, and make your own decisions.

The underlying value of all of this is the continued relationship building that occurs between you and your banker. Sure, the information you receive during these visits is good for your planning process, but it also maintains a link to an important personal contact.

When you get ready to do some strategic thinking, or are preparing to make some important decisions, remember to include your banker in the loop. Ask him for advice. It will make him feel important and appreciated.

Specific Strategy # 34

Ask your banker for advice.

> **Never hesitate to share your experiences with others.**

> **The most common mistake made by most small business owners is overestimating their sales.**

Explain That To Me One More Time

When you get ready to schedule a visit with your banker, have a specific purpose for the meeting. Whatever you do, don't drop in unannounced. Call for an appointment, and make sure the banker knows the reason for the visit. His time is important, just as yours is, so don't waste it. Have an agenda. It could be to review your third quarter numbers, discuss a new product line, evaluate a new competitor, or ponder a future business acquisition. There is absolutely no limit to your topics of discussion.

Be open and honest with your banker during these visits. Get right to the meat of the matter as far as what you think is going on in your business. And then, ask for his opinion and for his advice. Be willing to discuss your weaknesses as well as your strengths. By acknowledging your weaknesses and identifying how you will correct them, you will tremendously increase your credibility with your banker.

Solid information makes good memo material. And if there is one thing bankers have to do, it is to write detailed memos for every loan file. The better your banker knows you and what is going on in your business, the more accurate memo information will be placed in your loan file. Don't hold back. It is impossible to give a banker too much material. I will often have a loan applicant say, "I brought everything, because I didn't know what you would need." I reply, "Don't worry, I need it all."

You may have designed your own monthly management reports. Share copies of these with your banker. Copies of all your marketing materials, including brochures and ads, also help your banker in writing loan file memos. The more printed information you can provide, the easier you make it for your banker to accurately reflect your business in your ongoing loan file. Provide as much printed information as possible about your company and your industry. This will save a lot of time in writing those detailed memos to your loan file.

Specific Strategy # 35

Help your banker with his file memos.

CHAPTER 45

EXACTLY HOW DID YOU GET THIS JOB?

Interview your banker. Remember, you don't work for him; rather he is supposed to work for you. He didn't pick you. You picked him. You picked him to be your financial partner.

Your banker should work hard to help grow your sales and improve your bottom line. Is he willing to give you the time and attention to help make that happen? You should be able to think of your banker as your partner, and his actions and interest in your company should reflect that.

How long has he been a banker? Choose a lender with experience. How long has he been at the bank? You do not want to invest your time developing a relationship with someone, only to see him leave for another institution!

Does he have experience lending to your type of business? You don't have time to educate this guy. Is he easy to reach by phone? Are appointments required, and if so, can one be obtained that day?

Ask about educational background and personal interests. Find out as much as you can about this person. Before your loan is approved, your banker is going to know everything about you. Why shouldn't you know some things in turn?

Your banker should be your friend as well as your outside professional. Get to know your banker well enough to see if he has the potential to be a valued friend and confidant. If so, congratulations to you both.

Specific Strategy # 36

Your banker knows you, you should know your banker.

CHAPTER 46

YOU WANNA GO OUT SOMETIME?

Most bankers have favorite customers they entertain at ball games, concerts, dinners and such. A small nucleus of customers seems to benefit from this kind of attention. Why? I think it is because these people are the ones with whom bankers feel comfortable. We all enjoy socializing with people we know and accept for who we are. We can relax. Relationships are a building process. They really have to be worked in order to develop —they don't just happen.

You are the one who has the control in this aspect of your banking relationship. Remember, you have picked a banker whom you think you will enjoy on a social basis. You can control the depth of the relationship and how quickly it develops.

Put your banker on your invitation list to be invited to any social events you may attend. Always offer introductions to as many people as you can. Not only are you reinforcing your loyalty, you are helping your banker in networking some new business development leads. Wow! What a great idea.

Now you can call your banker again in a couple of weeks and say that you have arranged a lunch meeting to discuss banking needs with someone you introduced him to at a recent party. Guess what? You just got a free lunch. Your banker wins, too, because if you have provided a quality prospect, then he just picked up another quality customer, just like you.

Bottom line - don't wait for your banker to call you. Place a call now, and develop that relationship. You will find this amazingly easy to do.

Specific Strategy # 37

You control the development of the relationship with your banker.

SUMMARY

Strategy # 32
Negotiate terms and conditions after you get loan approval.

Strategy # 33
Don't overreact if you are turned down on a loan request.

Strategy # 34
Ask your banker for advice.

Strategy # 35
Help your banker with his file memos.

Strategy # 36
Your banker knows you, you should know your banker.

Strategy # 37
You control the development of the relationship with your banker.

“ **Yeah, I Want To Talk** ”
**With The President Of The Bank,
I Got Some Great Referrals
For Him!**

CHAPTER 47

TAKE MY KIDS...PLEASE!

It seems to bankers that every applicant who comes into the bank wants an unsecured line of credit for $50,000. One way to stay in good standing with your banker is to always be willing to provide collateral.

When the proper time comes or when circumstances dictate, your banker will actually suggest that the credit be extended on an unsecured basis. Be patient and wait for that day to arrive. You must allow the banker/borrower relationship adequate time to develop mutual trust.

Many borrowers believe that by giving their personal guarantee on a loan, it is secured by all of their assets, and should be approved based on the size of their net worth. This is not true. If your banker wants collateral on the loan, then it is necessary for you to specifically pledge an asset that would be available to the bank should you default on the loan. This is the banker's position here: "If the bank is willing to lend you the money, then you should feel comfortable enough with your ability to repay to put some of your personal assets at risk."

So, always be willing to offer collateral when it is available. It is not a good sign to your banker if you adamantly refuse to offer this kind of collateral. Do you want to give the impression that you have so little confidence in your ability to repay that you won't put your collateral at risk?

Be willing to offer a second mortgage on your home to your banker. Not only is it the best way of indicating to your banker that you are serious about adequately securing the loan, but under current tax laws, you may deduct the interest paid on the loan as well.

Even if your home is fully leveraged, which means that you do not have lendable equity in it, still offer it up as collateral. Even if your home is only a part of the collateral package, it may still be mortgaged by the bank to help reduce risk and ensure borrower commitment.

Many borrowers get confused when their banker discusses equity in their home versus lendable equity in their home. Equity is the difference between the fair market value and the indebtedness. Lendable equity is the difference between 80% of fair market value and the indebtedness.

Let's compare the differences on the same house with a market value of $100,000:

	A	B
Fair Market Value	$100,000	$100,000
80% Loan to Value		80,000
Debt on Property	- 60,000	- 60,000
	$ 40,000	$20,000
	Equity	Lendable Equity

Some borrowers think they can borrow the full $40,000 as shown in column A. Not so! While the 80% loan to value may vary from bank to bank, it is uncommon to be able to borrow 100% of the value of your home. As we have previously mentioned, you can try to get full advantage of all the equity in your home. This is likely to happen only if you were offering a larger collateral package, which could include other items, such as your business inventory and equipment.

Most small business owners will pledge the assets of their company, as well as a second mortgage on their home. This approach will usually provide an adequate collateral package for the bank and signals your total commitment to the repayment of the loan.

Success Strategy # 38

Be willing to offer collateral when it is available.

 " **Take Them. Really, I Don't Mind!** "

CHAPTER 48

YOUR BANKER AND YOUR SPOUSE WILL BE HAPPY

If you feel that your collateral package may be inadequate, here are some ways to correct it. Let's say that you are trying to borrow $100,000 for working capital in your business. How about offering a $100,000 life insurance policy on yourself to the bank? This can be a term policy with low premiums, which is not a great expense to you. It can very well be a policy that you already own; in that case, simply assign it to the bank. If you don't already have a $100,000 policy, then you are probably under-insured and need one anyway. This policy does not actually represent collateral to your banker, but it does offer a source of repayment in the event of your death.

As long as you are running your company, your cash flow is used to make loan payments at the bank. But if something happens to you, what happens to the cash flow? In many small businesses, it stops. Many times your spouse or even your business partner cannot generate the sales revenues that you did while you were alive. This results in an insufficient cash flow to make the loan payments.

Death benefits from your life policy will allow your company use of a windfall of working capital, which can make payments on your bank loan.

Specific Strategy # 39

You can always sweeten the collateral package with some cheap term insurance.

CHAPTER 49

Okay! Okay! My Word Is My Bond

If you are making an application for a loan in your company name, your banker will certainly require you to personally guarantee the debt. Many borrowers feel offended when asked to personally guarantee corporate debt because they feel the company should be able to "stand on its own."

Fortune 500 companies might be able to "stand on their own," but if you are not in that category - if your company stock is not publicly traded - then don't expect to borrow without offering a personal guarantee. Arguing with your banker about this point will only slow the approval process. This policy is universal - be prepared to deal with it wherever you go.

Your company assets usually consist of equipment, inventory and accounts receivable. Your banker will typically underwrite this type of loan request as if it were an unsecured loan. The normal loan-to-value on this collateral package is 50%. This means if you need $100,000 to invest in inventory you can expect to borrow only $50,000 from the bank.

This is a difficult type of loan to get approved at your local bank, because equipment, inventory and accounts receivable can quickly disappear when times get tough. Too many times, the inventory disappears before the bank realizes there was ever a problem.

When you sign a personal guarantee, you are not specifically pledging any of your personal assets. What you are saying is, "Hey, if the company goes belly-up, I will personally repay the loan so the bank will not lose any money."

If most of your personal assets are owned jointly with your spouse then offer your spouse's guarantee as well, even if the spouse is not involved in the business. You can improve your chances to get this type of loan approved by readily and willingly offering your personal guarantee and those of any other major shareholders.

Specific Strategy # 40

Always be willing to personally guarantee your business loans.

CASH IS KING AND I FEEL LIKE A JOKER

Cash is king! An adequate cash flow is extremely important in receiving loan approval. Many borrowers feel that as long as there is plenty of collateral, that the bank is not at risk. Well, collateral is just one of several requirements for loan approval. You must show that you have the ability to repay. You can do this by demonstrating to your banker that you have adequate cash flow to service your loan payments.

Some borrowers may say, "But you have a second mortgage on my home. It has $100,000 in equity. I only need to borrow $50,000." This only means the loan would be well secured. It doesn't mean you have shown adequate cash flow. The bank doesn't want your home, it only wants the monthly payments on a timely basis.

If you have taken any steps recently to improve your cash flow, be sure to tell your banker about them. Some examples: you renegotiated your office lease and decreased the monthly payments by $300. You recently reduced staff, resulting in an annual savings of $35,000 in personnel costs. You identified a new source for your raw materials to boost your gross profit margin by 3 percent.

Most borrowers can talk intelligently with their banker about securing the loan with adequate collateral. However, few borrowers can have that same conversation regarding their cash flow. In the banking business, we call this "capacity to repay." Debt service (or your monthly payments) comes from your cash flow. It does not come from your collateral. You must be prepared to review your cash flow worksheet with your banker and say, "As you can see, here is the money that will be available to make my loan payments."

Specific Strategy # 41

Cash flow, not collateral, repays loans.

500,000 REASONS

She wanted to borrow $500,000 and would offer as collateral a $500,000 certificate of deposit. I turned her down. Why would I turn down a loan that would be secured by cash collateral?

The loan request was for a start-up business. The $500,000 CD was being put up by a silent investor. I reviewed the business plan for the new company and had very little confidence that it could generate the projected sales.

Without adequate cash flow to make payments, the borrower would default on the loan. I would have to demand full payment on the loan and redeem the $500,000 CD to pay the loan balance.

At this point, the silent investor would become very active and hostile. Wouldn't you? The bank would almost certainly become entangled in the litigation between the borrower and the silent investor.

Evidence once again that you need cash flow, as well as collateral, to get your loan approved.

CHAPTER 51

I'M SO FLEXIBLE I CAN PUT MY FOOT IN MY MOUTH

We were sitting in my office discussing his application for two speculative home construction loans in a new subdivision. Home sales had begun to slow down, and I was hesitant to approve his loan request.

Sensing my hesitation, he said, "Look, I've been a spec builder for twenty years. If things get bad, I know how to get rid of a house. I'm flexible. I know how to adjust. I promise you that you won't ever get stuck with one of my houses."

That was all I needed to hear. I was already comfortable with all the other aspects of the credit application. I approved his loans. I was convinced this man could make a quick business decision when necessary.

As it turned out, things did get slow, really slow. But

the builder sold his houses and the bank got paid in full.

Small business owners must be able to make quick decisions. I have seen many business owners who were scared to make changes and failed because of it.

You must be flexible enough to make tough decisions that will create significant change. If the economy really slows down, can you lay off employees? Sell off assets? Adjust your standard of living? Are you willing to make these types of decisions in order to meet your credit obligations? Or will you sit on your problems, make no decisions and eventually be forced into bankruptcy?

If you have already performed these types of decision-making situations in the past, share them with your banker. If not, then explain to your banker that you know when to make the tough decisions and you are flexible enough to adapt to the changes.

Specific Strategy # 42

Always be prepared to make tough decisions.

CHAPTER 52

PLASTIC WON'T FLOAT FOREVER

Many small business owners have failed because they used credit cards to finance the company's start-up expenses. I have also seen business owners use their credit cards to help make payroll because the business couldn't afford it. One couple I know recently filed personal bankruptcy. They had charged $110,000 on dozens of personal credit cards, trying to keep their business afloat.

Don't drown in a sea of plastic. Credit cards should not be used to finance your business. The interest rates are far too high.

Access to capital is the number one problem facing small business owners. It is not only a problem when the company is doing poorly, but also when the company is doing well.

What? Sure! If business is booming and orders are flying in the door, where's the money to fill all those orders? This situation is referred to as "out growing your capital."

If your business is doing poorly, then you must scale down immediately, reduce your expenses as much as possible, and find out how to improve sales.

On the other hand, if your business is doing great and you are outgrowing your capital, you must make some equally tough decisions. Just remember - don't head to your credit cards as a source of capital.

Specific Strategy # 43

Never use credit cards for working capital in your business.

Summary

Strategy # 38

Be willing to offer collateral when it is available.

Strategy # 39

You can always sweeten the collateral package with some cheap term insurance.

Strategy # 40

Always be willing to personally guarantee your business loans.

Strategy # 41

Cash flow, not collateral, repays loans.

Strategy # 42

Always be prepared to make tough decisions.

Strategy # 43

Never use credit cards for working capital in your business.

" Plastic Won't Float Forever! "

CHAPTER 53

STAY IN TOUCH WITH YOURS

Be a thinker, and not just a doer. We are all guilty of getting caught up in the frantic day-to-day pace of running our business. We sometimes fail to step back to take a good, objective look at our company. Are we working smart? Do we have a target market? What is the quality of service? What is our competition doing?

Running your own company is usually a constant hot bed of stress. You wear many hats - marketing, sales, product development, personnel, financial planning . . . it goes on and on. As you grow in size, you are able to delegate some of these responsibilities, but the business is still your baby. You started it from day one, and you are the one who is ultimately responsible for it all.

As companies continue to grow, many owners may find less and less front line contact with customers. Stay on the cutting edge - keep yourself informed of your customers' needs.

I have seen many businesses fail because key employees leave, taking all the customers with them. This can easily happen when your key employees get to know your customers better than you do.

Customers having changing needs, and can offer you valuable advice that should be included in your business plan. Spend quality time with new customers, as well as long time customers. Take no one for granted. Ask your customers for ideas and remember to ask them for referrals. Your customers are your best source for new business leads.

Specific Strategy # 44

Bankers respect borrowers who stay in touch with their customers. Stay in touch with yours!

RED–HOT MAMA

"The lady on line two wants to speak to the president of the bank . . . and she's HOT!" my secretary whispered. I picked up the phone only to hear an irate customer scream, "I wrote a check for $200. I only had $190 in my account and you paid the check anyway."

I hesitated, then said, "You're mad because we paid the check. You mean you wanted us to return it?"

She was still fuming. "If I had wanted the check to be paid, I would have deposited $10 into my account," she hissed. "Never do that to me again!"

She slammed down the phone. I guess you never know what your customers want unless you ask them.

❝ If a bank customer says, ❞
"Oh, I'm just looking around,"
you better call the police.

❝ My grandfather would ❞
turn off his engine and coast
down hills in his '57 Ford Fairlane
to save gas... and my employees
think I'm tight?

SAY WHAT?!

As my bank continued to grow, I found I had less personal customer contact. My expanding staff was servicing the needs of our customer base. It seemed that I was only seeing those customers who had a problem or customers who specifically asked to see me personally (and those were surprisingly few).

Sensing this to be a problem, I decided to do something about it. I scheduled one-on-one employee meetings to get their input on different matters. At the time, I had about thirty-two employees. Over a two- week period, I invited each one to my office to discuss anything - their career, customer service, products, complaints, compensation- whatever. They set the agenda.

Each meeting averaged about forty-five minutes. I talked very little, listened very carefully, and took detailed notes. From that process, I learned a lot about what we were doing right and where we could improve. How? I was listening to the people in the organization who were with my customers every day, face to face. From these conversations, I developed a list of 201 ideas to improve the operation of our bank. Each idea would improve our profitability, morale or the quality of our customer service.

This process will work, for any size company. Even if you only have one salesperson, you still need to know what he is hearing from your customers. The comments he feels may not be important can be a signal to you that some changes are in order.

When you perform this exercise, be sure to share it with your banker. It will show that you are an open-minded listener who is not resistant to change. You can also get an opinion on the ideas you received.

Try it! I bet you can top my 200-plus list!

Specific Strategy # 45

Listening to your employees is as good as hiring a business consultant.

CHAPTER 55

DON'T TALK UGLY

Many times a new customer will walk into my office and tell me that he has left his old bank because of unfair treatment. This treatment usually turns out to be the denial of a loan request.

One of the worse things that you can do is to start badmouthing your ex-banker. When this happens, your new banker immediately becomes suspicious. Sure, there are some bankers out there who are not as smart as others. But for the most part, everyone operates by the same set of rules. It is the manner in which they abide by those rules that makes the difference.

When you start complaining about your old banker, your new banker will wonder how long it will take you to complain about him to yet another new banker. No one wants to enter a short term relationship with a disastrous ending!

This principle needs to be applied to all business relationships. When you call on a customer, never criticize your competition. Instead of concentrating on your opponent's weaknesses, you should promote your strengths.

If you are ending a relationship with one banker to form a new one, be completely honest about the reasons for the dissolution. The banking industry is a tightly-knit community, and its members share information. Your new banker will certainly call your ex-banker to get a credit reference on you. They will also talk in general about the nature of your previous relationship.

Tell your new banker that you are looking for a stronger relationship with a professional who has more time to service your banking needs. You may be leaving your old bank because of a specific reason: loan denial, misplaced deposits, returned checks. Whatever the reason may be, it could well have been avoided if you had developed a stronger relationship with your banker.

So, don't tell your new banker all the gory details. Just dwell on the fact that you need a personal banker who will appreciate your business.

Specific Strategy # 46

Never criticize and complain about your ex-banker.

CHAPTER 56

I'M NOT A NON-PROFIT...
I JUST LOOK LIKE ONE

Bankers are, for the most part, active community volunteers. Much of their new business is generated from networking efforts in civic and social clubs. It is a good idea for you to become involved in these activities as well for you may find your new banker there.

A special camaraderie develops among people who meet regularly in a civic or social organization. This type of interaction allows you to develop a special friendship with your banker that will transcend the normal banker/borrower relationship. Bankers work harder to get loans approved for a friend than for a mere acquaintance. So, use a charity to take your banker from a business relationship to a friendship.

Your participation in social and charitable activities also tells your banker a lot about your character. And your character is one of the primary areas that is considered by the banker while underwriting your loan.

Volunteer efforts also allow you to give something back to the community, and provides you a source of a new circle of friends you never would have made otherwise.

Specific Strategy # 47

**Share a membership
with your banker in a local civic club.**

DID YOU SAY BORED OR BOARD?

I have a good friend, Greg, a business consultant who specializes in teaching time management. His business is doing extremely well; in fact, he now sees the need to do some financial and estate planning to position himself for retirement. Greg also sees the need to plan strategically for continued growth to continue his hard-earned sales momentum.

I enjoy a close personal as well as business acquaintance with this gentleman. I have always encouraged him to use me as a resource for "thinking out loud" when planning ahead for his company. During a recent lunch meeting, he shared the following idea with me:

Greg had identified three people he wished to serve on his "board of directors." He planned to ask me, his CPA and his financial planner. This board would meet every six months to discuss his company's past performance, as well as future plans.

It is easier to make correct, timely decisions when others are present to help sort through the issues. As a small business owner, you can sometimes feel overwhelmed when important decisions are on the horizon. When it comes to your financial destiny, it's easy to wonder "How can I ever find the time to think about this, much less arrive at the correct solution, all by myself?" Yet, when you surround yourself with outside professionals, ones who want to help you, the solutions come much faster. These people can even help you identify what issues should be considered.

I quickly accepted Greg's offer to serve on his board. This was only an advisory position, offering no financial compensation or company equity. But I was flattered to be included in this important resource tool.

Specific Strategy # 48

**Flatter your banker.
Form a board of directors and ask him to serve on it.**

THE THREE WISE MEN

My friend, Greg, now refers to his board members as "The Three Wise Men." We meet every six months to discuss his company's performance and strategies. Why have I been so willing to accept his offer?

1. I am now ahead of any other banker in identifying his company's need for new loans. Therefore, I am not as worried about another banker "stealing" his business away from my bank.
2. I can help control the future growth and direction of his company.
3. It has strengthened my personal relationship with my customer.
4. The better I know Greg, his company, and his plans, the better I can serve him today.
5. Since I am familiar with his business plan, I am more comfortable loaning Greg money. I can more intelligently represent his interests during bank committee meetings.

Consider forming your own "board of directors." Prospects for your board can include anyone with whom you enjoy a business relationship. Consider the following:

1. Your banker
2. Your CPA
3. A supplier (Good idea if you get in a bind one day.)
4. Your spouse
5. Your mentor - the inspiration for starting you out on your own.
6. A peer (from a different trade area, of course)
7. A representative from your trade association
8. A key person on your management team (This is helpful if you plan to sell the business to him one day.)
9. Your best customer
10. Your attorney

If you only meet once every six to twelve months, these people will gladly give you their time. The compensation? A free lunch or dinner and a strengthened relationship with your company.

ONLY IF YOU LET ME BUY

Your banker is responsible for a very large portfolio of loans representing many millions of dollars. A loan portfolio of this size consists of hundreds of borrowers, certainly too many for the banker to schedule individual "quality time." Most of the time, the banker is putting out fires and taking care of those ever-present emergencies. These types of situations preclude the luxury of sitting back and reflecting, "Which of my loan customers should I take to lunch this week?" or "I should really play some golf or tennis with a customer on Saturday."

Well, what opportunity does this provide you? Call your banker to offer a lunch invitation. It is much easier for you to get around to making this call than it is for him. Look at it this way: your banker probably has a few hundred loan customers, but you only have one banker (OK, maybe you play it smart and have a couple.)

As you can see, the odds of you having a business lunch with your banker are much greater if you make the call. It isn't that your banker doesn't want to have lunch with you. It's just that his schedule is too frantic to arrange that lunch. Make that call - it's highly unlikely you'll be turned down.

Your banker probably has been assigned a certain number of business development calls to make each week. Congratulations! You have just helped make his job easier. Your name will certainly appear on his log sheet for calls he made that week. On top of that, he will probably insist that you let him pay since you are his customer. Don't argue; let him pay. If you have picked the right banker, then his expense account can certainly support it.

Will he ask you why you want to have lunch? Probably not. If he does, then say you just need some advice. Most of the conversation should center around you and your company.

Part of the small talk will certainly be about families. Listen carefully, because in follow-up phone calls, you will want to ask about family members by name. Personalizing the conversation in a genuine and caring manner will further strengthen your relationship with your banker.

A couple of days after the lunch, be sure to send a short, handwritten note. Highlight a good idea that he may have given you. He will save the note because they don't come very often. It is so amazing how the little things can make such a huge difference.

> **Specific Strategy # 49**
>
> **Call your banker and invite him to lunch.**

CHAPTER 59

TELL ME ONE MORE TIME HOW GOOD I AM

I throw away Christmas cards. I throw away letters. But I never throw away a handwritten thank you note recognizing something I did for somebody else. These notes make me feel good about myself. I call it my feel-good file.

A genuine compliment makes anybody feel good about themselves, whether it's expressed in a hand written note or a timely compliment.

Once a month, I sit and craft handwritten notes to people for things they said or did that merit recognition. I like to think these notes are saved as a source of inspiration for a day when things aren't going so great. It is impossible for anyone to ever receive too much praise or recognition.

You can certainly influence the attitude and performance

of others by praising them for doing an excellent job. I have several customers who send me handwritten notes praising me for things I do in the bank or in the community. When I see these customers, I get really pumped up and feel good about myself. This puts me in the mood to really go out of my way to help these people with their banking needs.

Use this strategy with your banker and see how the relationship improves. (Send some to your customers, too, while you're at it.)

Specific Strategy # 50

Send a handwritten thank you note to your banker.

SUMMARY

Strategy # 44
Bankers respect borrowers who stay in touch with their customers. Stay in touch with yours!

Strategy # 45
Listening to your employees is as good as hiring a business consultant.

Strategy # 46
Never criticize and complain about your ex-banker.

Strategy # 47
Share a membership with your banker in a civic club.

Strategy # 48
Flatter your banker. Form a board of directors and ask him to serve on it.

Strategy # 49
Call your banker and invite him to lunch.

Strategy # 50
Send a hand written Thank You note to your banker.

Review

Strategy # 1

Tell your banker that you will be a loyal customer.

Strategy # 2

It is best to be referred to the bank by a satisfied customer.

Strategy # 3

Always call tellers and other employees by name.

Strategy # 4

You must present yourself as an assertive and confident person with good communication skills.

Strategy # 5

A smile is your most valuable asset.

Strategy # 6

Be open and candid about your marital status or living arrangements.

Strategy # 7

How can I be a better customer?

Strategy # 8

Have passion and commitment for what you do.

Strategy # 9

Don't pick a bank, pick a banker.

Strategy # 10

Have plenty of patience if you are applying for a start-up business loan.

Strategy # 11
You should constantly emphasize your business experience.

Strategy # 12
Make a list of the financial needs you will require from your bank.

Strategy # 13
Make sure your banker knows that you understand and expect quality customer service.

Strategy # 14
You should schedule occasional visits with your banker when you don't need to borrow money.

Strategy # 15
Have an introductory visit with your banker before you apply for your loan.

Strategy # 16
Never rush your banker for a credit decision.

Strategy # 17
Invite your banker to your place of business.

Strategy # 18
Introduce your banker to your key employees.

Strategy # 19
Be a target customer for your bank.

Strategy # 20
Know what is on your credit bureau report.

Strategy # 21

Do everything you can to control the number of inquiries made to your credit bureau file.

Strategy # 22

Explain a credit problem to your banker before he finds out about it on his own.

Strategy # 23

If you have "perfect" credit always be sure to emphasize it early in the conversation with your banker.

Strategy # 24

Always call your banker before your payment becomes past due.

Strategy # 25

Always submit an honest and accurate personal financial statement.

Strategy # 26

Make sure you understand your financial statements well enough to discuss them with your banker.

Strategy # 27

Send your financial statements to the bank on a timely basis.

Strategy # 28

You must have a reliable written business plan.

Strategy # 29

Always take the time to prepare a "Written Loan Proposal."

Strategy # 30
Always prepare a realistic budget.

Strategy # 31
Write a short, easy-to-understand marketing plan.

Strategy # 32
Negotiate terms and conditions
after you get loan approval.

Strategy # 33
Don't overreact if you are turned down on a loan request.

Strategy # 34
Ask your banker for advice.

Strategy # 35
Help your banker with his file memos.

Strategy # 36
Your banker knows you, you should know your banker.

Strategy # 37
You control the development of the relationship
with your banker.

Strategy # 38
Be willing to offer collateral when it is available.

Strategy # 39
You can always sweeten the collateral package
with some cheap term insurance.

Strategy # 40
Always be willing to personally guarantee
your business loans.

Strategy # 41

Cash flow, not collateral, repays loans.

Strategy # 42

Always be prepared to make tough decisions.

Strategy # 43

Never use credit cards for working capital in your business.

Strategy # 44

Bankers respect borrowers who stay in touch with their customers. Stay in touch with yours!

Strategy # 45

Listening to your employees is as good as hiring a business consultant.

Strategy # 46

Never criticize and complain about your ex-banker.

Strategy # 47

Share a membership with your banker in a civic club.

Strategy # 48

Flatter your banker. Form a board of directors and ask him to serve on it.

Strategy # 49

Call your banker and invite him to lunch.

Strategy # 50

Send a hand written Thank You note to your banker.

Someone once said, "The first step is the hardest." If you do indeed want your banker to say "yes," then you have taken the first step by reading this book.

Now that you have gotten over this first hurdle, keep jumping! Reading my suggestions is one thing, but you must put them into motion. Define your course of action, make a list of bankers to contact, and get busy!

There is a banker out there who is ready to work with you. Whether it's a male banker or a female banker, it will be someone who will listen to your plans, help you develop sound strategies, and work with you to make them happen. But first you have to ask!

Remember, choose a banker, and not just a bank. Your relationship with your banker may be one of the most important keys to your business success. With your banker's support, you can open that new business, hire extra staff to meet customer demand, build an additional manufacturing plant, and more. Invite your banker to share your dreams, and make him a partner in your success.

Congratulations in your pursuit!

Index

A

ability to repay 157
accountant 117
accounts receivable 155
aerial photographs 134
affidavit 57
application 70
asset 52
asset quality 121
assumptions 125
attitude 49

B

basket 48
bend over backwards 24
board of directors 177
body language 51
bomb 17
"Boutique" banks 77
branch manager 17, 25
brochures 142
brokerage firm 29
budget 60, 71, 125, 126
business card 48
business consultant 172
business development calls 128, 182
business owners 21, 62, 76
business plan 60, 121

C

capacity 30
capacity to repay 158
car wash 45
cash flow 153, 157
cash flow worksheet 158
certificate of deposit 159
character 30, 108, 175
civic club 176
closing costs 131
collateral 124, 149, 150, 153, 157
collateral offered 30
collateral package 70, 150
comedy class 19, 20
communication 56
communication skills 50, 52, 56
community banker 66
community volunteers 175
confident 49, 50
consulting business 31
corporate 31, 32
counseling 137
CPA 115, 118, 177
credibility 44
credit bureau 99, 100
credit cards 163, 165, 166
credit history 30, 32, 107
credit report 100, 102, 108
credit risk 69
customer service representatives 23, 47
customers' needs 19

D

death benefits 154
debt service 158
default 149
Directors Loan Committee 134

divorce 55
due diligence 70

E

educational background 144
entrepreneurs 21
equipment 155
equity 71, 150
experience 70, 73, 74
extension fee 110

F

Fair Market Value 151
financial advice 137
financial information 60
financial statements 117, 118, 119
First Colony Bank Oath 23
forgery 57

I

interest rates 131
interview 78
inventory 71, 155

K

key employee 85, 168

L

late payment 104, 107, 109
lendable equity 150
leveraged 150
life insurance policy 153
line of credit 77
liquidity 70
loan application package 89
loan approval 55, 132, 157

loan committee 66, 90
loan file 142
loan limit 66
loan officer 47, 120
loan package 89
loan-to-value 151, 156
loyal customer 42
loyalty 42

M

management 85, 91
management reports 142
management tool 118, 125
managing partner 36
marital status 56
marketing committee 23
marketing materials 142
marketing plan 127, 128
medical community 19
memo 142
merger and acquisitions 121
minority-owned banks 77
mutual fund 81

N

narrative 74
net worth 149
networking 19, 46, 128, 146

O

operating costs 138
overhead 138

P

partner 36
passion 63, 64
payroll 87, 94

195

personal banker 67
personal financial statement 113, 115, 129
personal guarantee 149, 155
personnel costs 158
personnel file 24
podium 20
poultry house 133, 135
primary market area 127
production goals 132
prospect 146
public speaking 20

Q

quality service 26, 80, 82
Quality Service Award 24

R

real estate agent 19
real estate licensing course 19
realistic budget 129
realtor's needs 19
Red Hot Mama 169
referrals 43, 44, 59, 128, 168
relationship 65
repossessed 44
resumes 73, 124
retirement 35
risk 52, 69
risk analyzers 29, 70

S

sales projections 125
second mortgage 150
silent investor 159
silent partner 36
ski mask 34

smile 51, 52, 53
social events 146
social security numbers 123
source of repayment 153
speaking opportunities 20
start-ups 32, 35, 58, 69
strengths 142
stress 27, 83

T

target customer 97, 124
tax returns 124
teller 25, 47
teller line 18, 25
term insurance 154
Three Wise Men 179
Tire Changer 62
trends 138
Trick or Treat 111

U

unsecured 149

V

venture capital firm 36
visit 90

W

walk-in 86
weaknesses 142
working capital 35, 121, 154
written business plan 121, 122, 129
written loan proposal 123, 129

P.O. Box 707
Alpharetta, Georgia 30239-0707
(770) 569-8416
FAX (770) 667-9384

HUMOR HELP LINE!

Create Humor that Ken will share with others!
Please fill in the blanks.

A.) Ways to make your banker say yes . . .
   1. Tell him you enjoy visitors' day at the FDIC.
   2. _____
   3. _____

B.) It's hard to borrow money when . . .
   1. Your life is so messed up your mother won't co-sign.
   2. _____
   3. _____

C.) My payment was late because . . .
   1. I was busy balancing my checkbook.
   2. _____
   3. _____

Your donation of humor will help lift the spirits of others!
Thank you! For Acknowledgements. . .

Please Print Your Name_____

ORDER FORM

Fax Orders: (770) 667-9384

Mail Orders: PowerBanking Publications

P.O. Box 707

Alpharetta, Georgia 30239-0707

Phone Orders: (770) 569-8416

Have Your Visa or Mastercard Ready!

_____ cop(ies) "How To Make Your Banker Say Yes"
for $19.95 each $ _____

Georgia residents add $1.20 sales tax per book   _____

$2.50 shipping for first book,
75¢ each additional book   _____

Total Amount Enclosed $ _____

Company Name: _____

Name: _____

Address: _____

City _____ State _____ Zip _____

Telephone: _____

Payment: Check payable to PowerBanking Publications
        OR   Credit Card: ☐ Visa   ☐ Mastercard

Card Number: _____

Name on Card: _____ Exp. Date: _____

Please allow three to four weeks for delivery. Satisfaction guaranteed or you may return your book for a full refund.

P.O. Box 707
Alpharetta, Georgia 30239-0707
(770) 569-8416
FAX (770) 667-9384

HUMOR HELP LINE!

Create Humor that Ken will share with others!
Please fill in the blanks.

A.) Ways to make your banker say yes . . .
    1. Tell him you enjoy visitors' day at the FDIC.
    2. _____
    3. _____

B.) It's hard to borrow money when . . .
    1. Your life is so messed up your mother won't co-sign.
    2. _____
    3. _____

C.) My payment was late because . . .
    1. I was busy balancing my checkbook.
    2. _____
    3. _____

Your donation of humor will help lift the spirits of others!
Thank you! For Acknowledgements. . .

Please Print Your Name_____ _____

ORDER FORM

Fax Orders: (770) 667-9384

Mail Orders: PowerBanking Publications
P.O. Box 707
Alpharetta, Georgia 30239-0707

Phone Orders: (770) 569-8416

Have Your Visa or Mastercard Ready!

_____ cop(ies) "How To Make Your Banker Say Yes"
for $19.95 each $ _____

Georgia residents add $1.20 sales tax per book   _____

$2.50 shipping for first book,
75¢ each additional book   _____

Total Amount Enclosed $ _____

Company Name: _____

Name: _____

Address: _____

City _____ State _____ Zip_____

Telephone: _____

Payment: Check payable to PowerBanking Publications
      OR   Credit Card: ☐ Visa   ☐ Mastercard

Card Number: _____

Name on Card: _____ Exp. Date: _____

Please allow three to four weeks for delivery. Satisfaction guaranteed or you may return your book for a full refund.

P.O. Box 707
Alpharetta, Georgia 30239-0707
(770) 569-8416
FAX (770) 667-9384

HUMOR HELP LINE!

Create Humor that Ken will share with others!
Please fill in the blanks.

A.) Ways to make your banker say yes . . .
1. Tell him you enjoy visitors' day at the FDIC.
2. _____
3. _____

B.) It's hard to borrow money when . . .
1. Your life is so messed up your mother won't co-sign.
2. _____
3. _____

C.) My payment was late because . . .
1. I was busy balancing my checkbook.
2. _____
3. _____

Your donation of humor will help lift the spirits of others!
Thank you! For Acknowledgements. . .

Please Print Your Name_____

ORDER FORM

Fax Orders: (770) 667-9384

Mail Orders: PowerBanking Publications
P.O. Box 707
Alpharetta, Georgia 30239-0707

Phone Orders: (770) 569-8416

Have Your Visa or Mastercard Ready!

_____ cop(ies) "How To Make Your Banker Say Yes"
for $19.95 each $ _____

Georgia residents add $1.20 sales tax per book   _____

$2.50 shipping for first book,
75¢ each additional book   _____

Total Amount Enclosed $ _____

Company Name: _____

Name: _____

Address: _____

City _____ State _____ Zip_____

Telephone: _____

Payment: Check payable to PowerBanking Publications
              OR   Credit Card: ☐ Visa   ☐ Mastercard

Card Number: _____

Name on Card: _____ Exp. Date:_____

Please allow three to four weeks for delivery. Satisfaction guaranteed or you may return your book for a full refund.

P.O. Box 707
Alpharetta, Georgia 30239-0707
(770) 569-8416
FAX (770) 667-9384

HUMOR HELP LINE!

Create Humor that Ken will share with others!
Please fill in the blanks.

A.) Ways to make your banker say yes . . .
   1. Tell him you enjoy visitors' day at the FDIC.
   2. _____
   3. _____

B.) It's hard to borrow money when . . .
   1. Your life is so messed up your mother won't co-sign.
   2. _____
   3. _____

C.) My payment was late because . . .
   1. I was busy balancing my checkbook.
   2. _____
   3. _____

Your donation of humor will help lift the spirits of others!
Thank you! For Acknowledgements. . .

Please Print Your Name_____

ORDER FORM

Fax Orders: (770) 667-9384

Mail Orders: PowerBanking Publications

P.O. Box 707

Alpharetta, Georgia 30239-0707

Phone Orders: (770) 569-8416

Have Your Visa or Mastercard Ready!

_____ cop(ies) "How To Make Your Banker Say Yes"
for $19.95 each $ _____

Georgia residents add $1.20 sales tax per book   _____

$2.50 shipping for first book,
75¢ each additional book   _____

Total Amount Enclosed $ _____

Company Name: _____

Name: _____

Address: _____

City _____ State ____ Zip _____

Telephone: _____

Payment: Check payable to PowerBanking Publications

OR   Credit Card: ☐ Visa   ☐ Mastercard

Card Number: _____

Name on Card: _____ Exp. Date: _____

Please allow three to four weeks for delivery. Satisfaction guaranteed or you may return your book for a full refund.